A HOLIDAY Magazine
Travel Guide

IR

The *Holiday* Guide to

Prepared with the cooperation of the editors of HOLIDAY magazine.

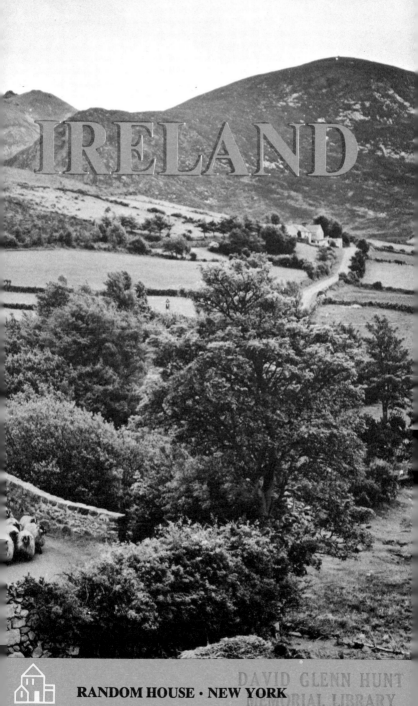

IRELAND

RANDOM HOUSE · NEW YORK

Photographs courtesy of the Irish Tourist Board

Cover Photograph: Goldman/FPG

Library of Congress Cataloging in Publication Data
Main entry under title:

The Holiday guide to Ireland.

(The Holiday magazine travel guide series ; 15)
Previous editions published under title: Ireland.
Includes index.
1. Ireland—Description and travel—1951-   —Guide-
books. 2. Northern Ireland—Description and travel—Guide-
books. I. Holiday. II. Series.
DA980.I54   1976   914′15′04′824   75–31767
ISBN 0–394–73195–6

Manufactured in the United States of America
2 4 6 8 9 7 5 3
Revised Edition

CONTENTS

CHAPTER 1

Back in the year 1577 a Dublin-born Englishman, named Richard Stanyhurst, listed the principal ingredients of Irishness in 22 succinct words. In his time they were, he testified,

> *"religious, franke, amorous, ireful, sufferable of infinite paines, very glorious, manie sorcerers, excellent horsemen, delighted with wars, great almsgivers, passing in hospitalitie".*

Barring the bit about sorcerers, this statement could stand today as a fair assessment of the Irish. A modern commentator would probably want to add "charming". Another might note the Irishman's keen sense of the ridiculous. And a third would almost certainly cite that native "Godawful gift of gab"—which actually has spawned poets, playwrights, orators and actors out of all proportion to the population, besides being responsible for the Irish wit and turn of phrase.

What makes the Irish what they are? No doubt their history, different from other European peoples, has done much to form their distinctive character. Ireland's past has been profoundly influenced by her geography. Much the same influence affects the Irish to this day.

Shaped like an elderly potato trailing sprouts, Ireland is about the size of Maine or South Carolina. To the east she is separated from Great Britain by the Irish Sea, which narrows in the south to St. George's Channel, opposite Wales. In the north the North Channel separates her from Scotland, at one point by only 13 miles. On its western flank Ireland is continuously subjected to two meteorological influences: the prevailing westerly winds

St. Finbarr's Cathedral and the River Lee, Cork

which circle the Northern Hemisphere at temperate latitudes, and the warm currents of the Gulf Stream. The winds bring clouds, made up of moisture from the ocean, while the Gulf Stream washes the western and southwestern coasts. As the clouds pass over these warm waters and the warmer land, condensation occurs and rain falls. Like the Pacific Northwest, similarly situated at the western edge of a northern continental landmass, Ireland gets plenty of rain; generally a drizzle. Mountainous parts in the west receive as much as eighty inches of rain a year. Dublin's annual rainfall, on the other hand, is no greater than New York's—between thirty and forty inches.

One result of Ireland's plentiful rain is the glowing rosy look of her people. Another is the soft, deep green of her countryside. First-time visitors to Ireland are rarely prepared for the latter phenomenon, however much they may have heard about it. But the "Emerald Isle" is, in fact, a perfectly accurate description.

Topographically, Ireland is often likened to a saucer; its undulating central plain is almost completely ringed by coastal highlands of varying geological structure. Most of the central plain is covered with bogs and with glacial deposits of sand and clay; its surface is dotted with hundreds of lakes. Ireland's biggest river, the Shannon, flows for 170 miles through the region, draining more than a fifth of the island. The south and southwest are characterized by old red sandstone rocks running roughly east and west, with limestone on the larger river beds. As one proceeds west, the ridges pile up into mountains, which reach their greatest heights in Ireland's southwest corner, County Kerry.

Apart from the pleasing sight of water and land and the constantly changing skyscapes, traveling in the central plain can be monotonous. But traveling anywhere else in Ireland is another matter: the landscape alters greatly at brief intervals and the traveler may have the illusion of visiting several countries in succession. Here is one of the charms of Ireland: the scenery is varied, distances are short, and the whole island is small enough to be visited in its entirety in a couple of weeks.

Ireland is made up of 32 counties. Historically, they are grouped in four provinces: Ulster (nine counties) in the north, Munster (six counties) in the south, Leinster (twelve counties) in the east, and Connacht, also spelled Connaught (five counties), in the west. But the only really significant political division today is that between the Republic of Ireland and Northern Ireland, known on both of its sides as "the border". The Republic—called both Ireland and its Gaelic (Irish) equivalent, Eire—consists of 26 counties, covering five-sixths of the island (27,073 square miles). Its capital is Dublin. The remaining six counties (5,451 square miles) comprise Northern Ireland. Often some-

An Aer Lingus plane stops at Cork Airport

what inaccurately called Ulster, and usually referred to, south of the border, as "the Six Counties". Northern Ireland, like Scotland and Wales, is an integral part of the United Kingdom. Of Ireland's total population of 4,528,000, about two thirds live in the Republic (2,979,000) and a third live in Northern Ireland (1,549,000). Thus, Northern Ireland is more than twice as thickly populated as the 26 Counties—reflective of the dominance of industry in the northeast and of agriculture elsewhere.

The political partition of Ireland reflects a deeper split, between Catholic and Protestant Irishmen. As Stanyhurst and many others after him have noted, the Irish are an intensely religious people. Ireland's Catholics, in particular, are noted by other Catholics for their devotion to the Faith. In the Republic they make up no less than 95 per cent of the population. In Northern Ireland, however, the Protestants (Presbyterians, Church of Irelanders, Methodists, and others) are twice as numerous as the Catholics, who nevertheless predominate in a good many of the rural areas. Unfortunately, political and economic inequities have grown out of this religious division, and (despite a supposedly binding truce between the two groups symbolized by the white band in the flag), violence and bloody riots have been disrupting Northern Ireland since 1970. British troops moved in to quell the fighting, furthering the resentment of the Catholic minority which resurrected its own army. Both sides are now firmly entrenched in this age-old struggle, and the ideal of a united Ireland seems farther away than ever.

To many American visitors, of course, Ireland is the "old sod"; they are drawn there by mystical tides of kinship, in pursuit of their heritage and, in a sense, of themselves. But a large and steadily increasing number of visitors bring not a drop of Irish blood across the Atlantic. They come with any of many purposes in mind. They may want to inspect a few of the tens of thousands of field monuments from past ages—which generations of superstitious farmers and shepherds have allowed to leave standing; or to visit some of the elegantly beautiful Georgian houses, in city and country. Perhaps they plan to retrace the footsteps of Swift, Shaw, Wilde, Yeats, Joyce, or some other favorite Irish writer, or watch the world-famous Abbey Theatre players in action. Again, they may want to fish in Ireland's uncrowded and unspoiled lakes and rivers, or in the warm waters off the coast where sharks and other deep-sea denizens disport themselves. They may want to tramp through wild, romantic Connemara, or visit the starkly beautiful Aran Islands, where Gaelic survives as a native tongue, or make a leisurely circuit, in a gypsy cart pulled by a horse, of the fabled Ring of Kerry. Or they may be attracted to that most glamorous of international equestrian events, the Dublin Horse Show, to the countless country fairs, or to the weeks-long annual festivals put on by the major cities. They may plan to ride to hounds or take a leisurely pleasure cruise down the lordly Shannon; stay a while in a Norman castle or shop for Irish lace, linen, knitwear, or glassware. They may simply wish to sample a pint of Guinness and conversation in a genuine Irish pub, so utterly unlike those in American cities. Or they may . . . but the list could go on and on. For Ireland is truly a country of *multum in parvo,* of "infinite riches in little room". And, we might add, at comparatively little cost.

But for many an American or Canadian, the greatest attraction of a visit to Ireland is simply the change of pace it affords. Time itself seems to slow down in unhurried Ireland, where the weather never reaches extremes and unspoiled, beautiful scenery surrounds him tensions and troubles melt into the misty air. The people he meets can have lots to do with this regenerative process —for the Irish are today, just as their ancestors were four centuries ago, "passing in hospitalitie".

CHAPTER 2

Thousands of years ago, the huge ice sheet that had covered all Ireland began to melt and withdraw to the north, scooping out lakes and piling up mountains in its wake. Around 6000 B.C. settlers arrived, probably by way of the land bridge which then linked Ireland to Britain. Little is known of these people except that they made flint tools and lived by hunting and fishing. After the land bridge was severed these Stone Age folk survived in settlements by lakes and rivers until the rise, before 2000 B.C., of a culture based on farming and cattle raising.

These Neolithic men and women made pots and bowls, lived in round and rectangular houses. They cremated their dead, interring the ashes and charred bones under stone cairns or in burial chambers inside earthen tumuli. A number of these constructions survive, a few still awaiting excavation. The best known, excavated and open to visitors, is a large tumulus, covering a full acre, near *Newgrange,* County Meath.

With the dawn of the Bronze Age, some time after 2000 B.C., came the manufacture of implements and ornaments of copper and gold, the latter metal then being abundant in the mountain streams of what is now County Wicklow. The tin needed for bronze, not being present in Ireland, was imported from Cornwall. Gold ornaments of Irish provenance played an important role in overseas trade, perhaps even serving as currency; examples have been found in many parts of Britain and in northern France, Denmark, and Luxembourg.

From the few human bones found on Irish Bronze Age sites anthropologists have deduced that the inhabitants were of the

Mediterranean type—relatively short and somewhat swarthy-skinned. Beginning in the fourth century B.C. these people were joined by the Celts. The Celtic newcomers, who originated between the headwaters of the Rhine and the Danube, had by that time spread westward, gradually subduing the people north of the Alps. They came to Ireland, initially, in small numbers. But a superior military organization and iron weaponry enabled them, in following migrations, to conquer the indigenous people. Later they imposed on them their language, the basis of Gaelic, along with a system of small kingdoms.

At the start of the Christian era the Celtic states of Ireland were consolidated in five kingdoms. Two and a half centuries later Cormac Mac Airt, High King of Tara, emerged as the most imposing ruler in the land, and by the end of the sixth century the Tara Monarchy was paramount. By that time Ireland, too, had become Christian. St. Patrick arrived in the year 432, and Christianity spread rapidly. In 563 St. Columcille (Columba) established monastic settlements at *Iona,* and Ireland soon became an important educational and religious center. During the ensuing centuries many thousands of students flocked to the great monastic schools of Ireland, while Irish missionaries carried religion and learning to distant parts of Europe.

Toward the end of the eighth century, Norse sea-rovers began to harry Ireland's coasts, killing, looting, and pillaging. In 841 the Danes planted a settlement at the mouth of the River Liffey which was to grow into modern Dublin. The Vikings' power was not finally broken until 1014, with their defeat at *Clontarf* by the celebrated warrior-king Brian Boru. Their depredations caused immense havoc but, on the other hand, they forced the loosely-knit society, known as the Gaelic Order, to adopt sounder economic patterns and also a new feeling of nationhood.

In 1170, a little more than a hundred years after their conquest of England, the Normans invaded Ireland. (This marked the beginning of the cross-channel struggle that was to continue into the present century.) In time, many Normans adopted the Irish language and Irish ways, becoming, in effect, Irish themselves. But English monarchs successively strove to impose their will on the people of Ireland, Gaels and Norman-Irish alike. Their efforts culminated in a decisive English victory at *Kinsale,* in 1602. The subsequent flight of the defeated Irish chieftains to the Continent spelled the demise of the old Gaelic Order. The way was open to large-scale seizures of property where the English thereafter planted colonies of Protestants loyal to their cause.

In the middle of the seventeenth century, following the Puritans' triumph in England's Civil War, Oliver Cromwell arrived in Ireland to institute a campaign of repression. To the cry of "To Hell or Connacht!" the invaders forced the Irish landowners to flee to the barren west or die; their lands were parceled out among the conquerors. With the restoration of the Stuart monarchy in 1660 conditions improved somewhat, and when Charles II was succeeded in 1685 by his outspokenly Catholic brother, James II, the Irish rejoiced. For three years Ireland was virtually a Catholic kingdom. But in 1688 the English Parliament deposed James in favor of the Dutch Protestant, William of Orange; James fled to France, and the following year arrived in Ireland, where he raised an army. In 1690, however, King William, at the head of a Protestant and Anglo-Dutch army, roundly defeated James's Catholic and Franco-Irish forces in the Battle of the Boyne. James again fled to France, leaving the Irish to their fate. The next year, after a prolonged seige, the last Jacobite resistants capitulated to William at *Limerick*.

The victor offered comparatively generous terms, including the right of the Irish in the five western counties to retain both their religion and their land. Parliament, however, was determined to strengthen the Protestant ascendancy in Ireland; its members refused to ratify the Treaty of Limerick. More lands were seized, in what amounted to the third wholesale confiscation in a century.

Moville, Co. Donegal, on Lough Foyle, with Northern Ireland beyond

An evocative ruin, Tintern Abbey, Co. Wexford

Between 1695 and 1727 Parliament enacted a series of oppressive measures aimed at Ireland's Catholics, who, then as now, constituted the great majority of the people. These acts, known collectively as the penal laws, deprived Catholics of all civil and political rights. Catholics could not sit in Parliament or vote; they were barred from the professions and forbidden to educate their children, either at home or abroad. The peasants lived in dire poverty, but some Catholic aristocrats, protected by their social position, retained their lands.

To the outraged Irish, the Treaty of Limerick had not simply been repudiated, but violated. This betrayal remains to many Irishmen a heinous instance of treachery on the part of "perfidious Albion".

In time the transplanted Anglo-Irish Protestants came more and more to identify with Ireland. By the second half of the eighteenth century a Protestant patriot party arose, ultimately under the leadership of Henry Grattan, to demand greater independence. This led to the establishment, in 1782, of an independent Irish Parliament in Dublin. Effective power, however, still rested in the hands of the English. During the tenure of "Grattan's Parliament" Dublin grew into a capital of fine buildings and noble squares; but the Catholic peasants of the countryside remained as wretched as ever.

A truly democratic movement arose in 1790 with the foundation of the Society of United Irishmen. The founder, a young Protestant lawyer Theobald Wolfe Tone, was inspired by the French Revolution. The United Irishmen adopted a revolutionary program and planned a national uprising which took place in 1798. They received French aid, but were ill-armed and badly led and were crushed. Wolfe Tone, caught and condemned to death, committed suicide.

Two years later, over the strong protests of Grattan and the patriots, a suborned Irish Parliament accepted an Act of Union previously enacted at Westminster, and Ireland formally entered the United Kingdom. However, in 1803 Robert Emmet, another patriotic young Protestant, led an insurrection even more disastrous than Wolfe Tone's, only to be hanged for his pains.

Meanwhile, the gradual relaxation of the penal laws had allowed some Catholics to receive an education; one, a young lawyer from County Kerry named Daniel O'Connell, began to agitate for Catholic emancipation. In 1823, with some brilliant young helpers he formed a Catholic association, financed by dues of a penny a month. Five years later he stood for Parliament for County Clare—as a Catholic who could not take his seat until the anti-Catholic oath was set aside. His triumphant election enabled the parliamentary liberals to carry the Emancipation Act of 1829, whereby Catholics were admitted to Parliament, and to most public offices.

Known as "The Liberator", O'Connell for years pressed for the repeal of the Union with Great Britain. His efforts failed, and his leadership was gradually taken over by younger men of the Young Ireland movement. Before they could accomplish much, however, Ireland was prostrated by the most frightful calamity of her long and troubled history: the potato blight and the famine that followed it.

For reasons traceable for the most part to English economic policy, Ireland had become largely dependent on a single crop, potatoes. In 1846, when a then little-understood plant disease ruined Ireland's potato crop, the country's population stood at over eight million; in just four years, starvation and emigration had reduced this figure to six million, and in the next half century continued emigration, mainly to the United States, reduced it to half the pre-famine level.

Political activity continued. In 1848 the Young Irelanders staged a rebellion. This was soon put down and leadership passed to another revolutionary group, the Irish Republican Brotherhood, known as the Fenians. In 1867 the Fenians, aided by generous contributions from Irish-Americans, rose against the English. But they, too, were crushed.

Then, in 1869, a Protestant lawyer named Isaac Butt founded the Home Rule Party, with the object of obtaining autonomy for Ireland. Three years later a strong contingent of Home Rulers entered the British House of Commons; the following year the party's leadership passed to one of Ireland's heroes, Charles Stewart Parnell. Parnell remained the chief champion of Home Rule until 1890, when his involvement in a divorce suit wrecked his position and split his party. A year later Prime

Minister Gladstone, who had done much for the Irish peasants through various land acts, achieved the passage of a Home Rule Bill through the House of Commons, only to see it rejected by the Lords.

In 1905 Arthur Griffith, a Dubliner who had started his working life as a printer and gone on to found a remarkable political and literary paper, the *United Irishman,* formed a movement which came to be known as "Sinn Fein", Gaelic words meaning "ourselves" and implying the idea of "standing alone". The Sinn Fein sought an independent Ireland under the Crown; to this end, Sinn Feiners elected to Parliament refused to go to Westminster and convened in Ireland instead, as a sort of unacknowledged government of Ireland. The movement rapidly gained momentum, leading to the formation in 1913 of a patriotic army, the Irish Volunteers.

In 1914 Great Britain was at war and thousands of Irishmen enlisted in the British Army. To the astonishment of the world, including the Irish, rebellion broke out in Dublin on Monday of Easter Week, 1916: a small group under the unlikely leadership of a gentle schoolmaster-poet, Patrick Pearse, and a labor leader, James Connolly, seized two key public buildings and proclaimed Ireland a republic. Within a week the Easter Rebellion was crushed; Pearse, Connolly, and fourteen other patriot leaders were executed, and hundreds of rebels were either deported or imprisoned. As the poet Yeats was to write of the event, "A terrible beauty was born."

Dunguaire Castle, Co. Galway, has seen much history

The American Embassy in Ballsbridge, Dublin

The Easter Rising was an absurd project—foredoomed to failure—yet it did galvanize the Irish people and, in the long run, its objectives were attained: For in 1919, with the return of peace in Europe and the release of the Easter uprising veterans, the Irish struggle for freedom was renewed. Britain attempted to suppress the guerilla fighting with a force of mercenary soldiers; the Irish called them the Black and Tans, after the colors of their uniforms. After two years of guerilla warfare, the Anglo-Irish Treaty was signed in 1921—setting up the Irish Free State of 26 counties within the British Empire.

However, the more radical elements, led by Brooklyn-born Eamon de Valera, would settle for nothing less than an independant republic. For two more years Ireland was wracked by sanguinary strife between supporters and opponents of the Treaty. The Free State government proved strong enough to endure, and in 1923, the IRA called off armed resistance. Three years later de Valera and his followers founded the Republican Fianna Fail party. In 1932 the Fianna Fail took office. The Irish government abolished the oath of allegiance to the Crown and stopped paying Britain interest on loans contracted under various land acts. This last move provoked an economic war between Britain and Ireland, not resolved until 1938. Ireland then agreed to pay Britain £10,000,000 in lieu of the annuities, and Britain agreed to give up the naval bases she had retained in Ireland under the Anglo-Irish Treaty.

When war broke out in Europe, the 26 Counties proclaimed their neutrality. Northern Ireland, as a part of the United Kingdom, automatically became a combatant. She built fighter planes for the R.A.F. and the shipyards of Belfast turned out ships for the Royal Navy. Londonderry (always called Derry south of the border and by anti-Unionists north of it) was the site of a large U. S. Navy base, where hundreds of American vessels made port after convoying men and supplies across the Atlantic. Although Premier de Valera resisted the pressures of Churchill and Roosevelt to join in the war, tens of thousands of Irishmen again volunteered for the British armed forces.

By first post-war general election, in 1948, the Fianna Fail no longer commanded a clear majority so a coalition government was formed, under John A. Costello. The new government announced Eire's secession from the British Commonwealth and the following year Ireland became an independent nation.

Six years later, Ireland joined the United Nations. There she has played a far more important role than would seem the lot of so small and relatively poor a country. Such brilliant spokesmen as Conor Cruise O'Brien have undoubtedly helped.

During the early 1960s two men greatly influenced the Irish— Pope John XXIII and President John F. Kennedy. Although the liberal pontiff unquestionably irked some of the conservative Irish Catholic clergy, the man himself was loved deeply. As for the young President, he was "one of their own". His picture still hangs over the bar in many pubs. The Irish people's grief at his death was only blunted by the tragedy that has overtaken Northern Ireland in the 1970's.

Throughout this century, the population of Ireland has remained fairly static, increasing only slightly. The reasons for this are primarily economic, secondarily religious. Not many years ago an Irish farmer put off marrying until his middle years, when, on his father's death, he would inherit enough land to support a wife. With the economic picture improved the average age for marrying has dropped somewhat, but it is still high. And, while the total of Irish bachelors has decreased, the percentage of Irishmen who elude marriage—either through dread of poverty, sex, or of making a bad match which only death could undo—is greater than any western country. The paucity of opportunity has forced young people to seek a better life elsewhere. In this century emigration has been mainly to Britain, especially to London, Liverpool, and the industrial cities of the north. Many of the emigrants have been women, with the result that the female population of Ireland is now smaller, relatively, than it is in most countries.

Ireland's birth rate now exceeds her death rate by a healthy margin and hopeful signs point to the slowing down of emigration. The government's sustained effort to attract foreign capital to Ireland has met with considerable success: British, American, German, and other companies have set up factories and processing plants, in both the cities and rural areas with the result that young people have been able to find employment close to home instead of being forced to join the drift to Dublin or overseas. To cite two examples of recent progress, Ireland's second city, Cork, now boasts an extensive waterside international industrial complex, and also plays host to the world each year at an international film festival. And the Shannon Free Airport Development Co., a body part-governmental and part-private, has persuaded firms to set up shop in the region, thus bringing a measure of prosperity to the southern tier of County Clare by the Shannon estuary.

Along with the growth of industry has come a tremendous increase in tourism, which now ranks as the country's second earner of foreign exchange. This increase has come about largely through the efforts of the Irish Tourist Board, Aer Lingus, the national airline, and government agencies. The Board has supplied hoteliers and caterers with generous grants to enable them to improve their establishments. It is worth remembering, though, that Irish tourism could hardly have boomed as it has if the country did not possess so much to offer the visitor—and at prices lower than most European countries.

Before the big race—the Parade Ring, the Curragh, Co. Kildare

CHAPTER 3

WHAT YOU SHOULD KNOW ABOUT IRELAND

Flying over Ireland quickly confirms that the country is made up for the most part of farms. Brown peat bogs, from which the Irish obtain fuel for both home fires and power plants, cover about four per cent of the country. There are few wooded patches to be seen: only about one-fortieth of the land is under trees, an imbalance which is being corrected through a national forestry program. Roads wind across the lovely green countryside, linking tiny hamlets and small, compact towns. The fields, taking their cue from old patterns of land-division, and also, one suspects, from an ingrained Irish distaste for too much regularity, stretch away in all directions, no two the same shape and size. The fences separating them are mainly of gray stones in the less-fertile west, and of hedgerows elsewhere.

Arriving in just about any Irish town or city, except Dublin, is for many Americans like being whisked back to childhood. Few buildings are more than four stories high. The skyline is dominated only by church spires or cathedral towers. Probably there's a whiff of coal-smoke in the air, mingled with aromatic peat-smoke. In the streets, which also rarely follow a straight line, there is less traffic than in American towns; though drivers move along at a good clip, they must be ready to slow down to the pace of the horse-drawn cart which may, at any moment, emerge from a side street. The urban buses, of the majestic double-decker variety, look improbably vast as they lumber past the rows of neat, brightly-colored shop fronts.

Traveling through the Irish countryside is like being transported through an enchanted toyland. Farmhouses, barns, fields—even cars and trucks—all seem to have been constructed on the same Lilliputian scale. The very landscape appears to conform to this pattern; a good many of what the Irish call mountains would be called hills in the United States or Canada. Altogether, if it were not for the presence of perfectly normal-sized Irish citizens one could easily imagine that Ireland was literally the home of the "little people". This old-fashioned atmosphere existing in a small-scale environment, plus the charm and spirit of the Irish themselves, can hardly fail to enchant the visitor.

WHEN TO GO

May is usually the sunniest month in the north, west, and midlands of Ireland; elsewhere, June generally has the most sunshine. July, or in some places August, is the warmest month, with temperatures averaging between 58° and 60°. Thanks to the moderating influence of the Gulf Stream it hardly ever gets really cold in Ireland: in February, the coldest month, temperatures average between 40° and 42°. Snow hardly ever falls except in the high mountains.

Many travelers prefer to visit Ireland in the spring and fall, when there are not so many other tourists around: in April, showers alternate with bright sunshine, while in late September and October the weather is often crisp and clear. Incidentally, showers may coincide with sunshine at any season, producing magical rainbows.

One of Eire's prettiest villages—Adare Village, Co. Limerick

Because Ireland lies so far to the north—at approximately the same latitude as Labrador—summer days are long and winter days short. In June, daylight lasts until 10 o'clock or later, while in December darkness falls as early as 4 in the afternoon.

But weather factors are not the only criteria of when to go to Ireland. There is the matter of expense. During the off-season —roughly October through May—air and sea fares are low. So are the rates charged by hotels, guesthouses, and car-hire firms. On the other hand in summer there is more going on: festivals and fairs, sports and outdoor recreation. Also the services of the government-run airlines, railways, and bus lines are more extensive.

TRAVEL DOCUMENTS

Americans and Canadians need no visas to enter Ireland; all they need is a valid passport. Travelers proceeding to the United Kingdom or arriving from there are not even required to show their passports. A certificate of vaccination against smallpox is no longer necessary for re-entry into the United States. Inquiries regarding a protracted stay should be addressed to a consulate of the Republic of Ireland; or, in Northern Ireland, to a British consulate.

PLANNING YOUR TRIP

Possibly as a consequence of unwelcome incursions by Vikings, Normans and Englishmen, the Irish possess a high regard for privacy. A visitor who prefers to keep to himself can be sure that his wishes will be respected. However, the Irish are largely an outgoing lot, who like nothing better than to strike up a conversation with a stranger. If he is American or Canadian, so much the better: most Irishmen have relatives or friends on this side of the Atlantic, and many have spent some time here themselves.

Since the Irish people are also "passing in hospitalitie", an encounter can easily lead to a personally conducted tour of local places of interest, including pubs, and/or an invitation home to dinner. This may throw carefully laid plans out of kilter. Some travel writers recommend that visitors avoid committing themselves to rigid itineraries before they set foot in Ireland. Instead, they are counseled to adopt the planless "method" of Laurence Sterne, the great eighteenth-century Irish novelist and traveler, as set forth in his marvelous account *A Sentimental Journey*.

But not all travelers enjoy "playing it by ear". There is, too, the crucial matter of time. Because Ireland lies nearer New York, Boston or Montreal than any other part of Europe, many travelers visit it at the beginning or end of their European tour. Sometimes this means that their stay in Ireland is limited to a few days. They want to see as many of Ireland's attractions as possible and who can blame them?

There is no shortage of interesting books for background reading on Ireland. There are, to begin with, the works of Ireland's foremost twentieth-century novelists, short-story writers, poets and playwrights—men like William Butler Yeats, James Joyce, J. M. Synge, James Stephens, Sean O'Casey, Oliver St. John Gogarty, Padraic Colum, Brendan Behan, and Patrick Kavanagh. While familiarity with these authors is not essential to understanding their homeland, it gives insight to the Irish character and Irish scene. In a lighter vein, the humorous novels of Flann O'Brien and Honor Tracy pinpoint Irish idiosyncracies and the ability of some Irishmen to poke fun at their countrymen's foibles. But this latter must never be mistaken for a national trait: Miss Tracy's riotous sketches of rural Irish life, in particular —drawn from the viewpoint of a member of the Anglo-Irish Protestant "elite"—arouse, in the breasts of many a patriot, feelings of wrathful indignation, something like those which prompted a Dublin mob to break up the opening of Synge's *Playboy of the Western World* more than half a century ago— on the grounds it was a vile slander on the fair name of Ireland.

As for information on Ireland, any good-sized bookstore is a likely source. The scenic beauty of Ireland has drawn many top photographers and fascination with the Irish character has inspired floods of print. One modest but excellent description of Ireland, written by a young Bostonian couple William and Constance Kehoe, is *Enjoying Ireland* (Devin-Adair Company, New York, 1966). In Ireland, two paperbacks together give a complete picture of the country. They are *Facts About Ireland,* published by the Department of Foreign Affairs, and the *Illustrated Ireland Guide,* published by the Irish Tourist Board.

The Irish Tourist Board—whose Gaelic name, *Bord Failte Eireann,* means literally "Irish Board of Welcomes"—is equipped to answer any question you may have about the country. In the United States, Irish Tourist Board offices are located at 590 Fifth Avenue, New York, N. Y. 10036 (Telephone [212] 246-7400); 135 South La Salle Street, Chicago, Ill. 60603 (Telephone [312] 726-9356/7/8); 681 Market Street, San Francisco, Cal. 94015 (Telephone [415] SU 1-5688); and 510 West Sixth Street, Los Angeles, Cal. 90014 (Telephone [213] 624-8961).

Bord Failte's head office is at Baggot Street Bridge, Dublin 2. In addition, there are eight regional tourism organizations, covering the entire Republic and working in liaison with Bord Failte. The many offices of these organizations are staffed by helpful, friendly people who know their regions well.

For information on travel to and in Northern Ireland, inquiries should be addressed to the offices of the British Tourist Authority. In the U. S. and Canada, these are at 680 Fifth Avenue, New York, N. Y. 10019 (Telephone [212] 581-4700; 875 North Michigan Avenue, Chicago, Illinois 60611 (Telephone [312] 787-0490), 612 South Flower Street, Los Angeles, Cal. 90017 (Telephone [213] 623-8196); 151 Bloor Street West, Toronto M5SIT3, Ont. (Telephone [416] 925-6326).

The Northern Ireland Tourist Board publishes a descriptive paperback book entitled *The Ulster Guide* and issues a glossy-paper annual, *Northern Ireland.* The Board's principal tourist center is in River House, 48 High Street, Belfast (Telephone Belfast 31221), with a branch office at Belfast Airport (Alder-grove), or write the British Tourist Authority offices in London, at 64 St. James' Street, S.W.1A or New York at 680 Fifth Avenue.

Rugged Inisheer, Aran Islands, Co. Galway

Bantry Bay, Co. Cork, in Ireland's glorious Southwest

HOW TO GET THERE

Three international airlines schedule regular flights from the U. S. and Canada to Shannon Free International Airport and to Dublin.

By sea. There are no longer any passenger ships sailing between the United States and Ireland. People with lots of time and a taste for shipboard life will have to disembark at Southampton, in England, and make their way overland to Ireland.

By air. Aer Lingus and T.W.A. operate daily flights from points in North America to Shannon and Dublin. Only Aer Lingus, however, flies jets direct to Dublin from cities other than New York. Air Canada flies to Shannon only.

Air fares are steepest during the peak periods of travel, that is, during June, July, and August. Fares are the same on all scheduled airlines.

The most economical fare—the APEX (Advance Purchase) 22 to 45-day round-trip excursion from New York to Shannon costs $382 in peak season, and $285 in the low season (November through March). Those same fares rise to $476 and $345 respectively for a regular 22–45 day trip.

The 14 to 21-day round-trip excursion is considerably more expensive. From New York to Shannon in peak season it costs $543, in low season $455. From New York to Dublin, this fare is $561 and $473, respectively.

From fall to spring, there are eight-day packages which cost $318 for round-trip air fare from New York to Shannon and a minimum of $70 land expenses including car rental and first-class hotel accommodations.

A one-way ticket (Shannon–New York)—for those staying longer than 45 days or less than a week—costs $347 or $262 depending on season.

Many reasonably priced package tours are available from travel agents. These include your round-trip flight, two weeks in the best hotels, meals, excursions and entertainment. Some include the rent of a car, unlimited rail travel, or a conducted bus tour.

Youth fares, 30–35% cheaper than standard fares, are offered by most airlines to those under 22. Children under 12 usually fly half fare if accompanied by their parents.

Information regarding flights to and from Ireland and a great deal more—including all-in tours of the country (at astonishingly low prices)—can be obtained at the offices of Irish International Airlines. (*Aer Lingus,* the airline's Gaelic name, means "Air Fleet".) In addition to Shannon, Dublin, Cork and Belfast, Irish-Aer Lingus serves London, Manchester and other large cities in Britain. It also has scheduled flights from Shannon and/or Dublin to Paris, Madrid, Brussels, Dusseldorf, Frankfurt, Munich, Rome, Geneva, Zurich, Amsterdam and Copenhagen, serving, altogether, 34 destinations. The Irish-Aer Lingus people will gladly help you to set up an itinerary taking in Ireland and other countries of Western Europe. (Travel agents can, of course, do the same.)

Every shamrock-tailed Irish-Aer Lingus plane bears the name of an Irish saint on its nose. Each year the entire fleet is blessed at Dublin Airport by a priest who commends planes, crews and passengers "into the hands of God and the special protection of

Connemara cottages in Rossaveal, County Galway.

Knappogue Castle, Co. Clare, scene of medieval banquets

Mary, Mother of God". They must be doing something right, for in a third of a century of operations the airline has piled up a safety record rival airlines may well envy. In any case, and for whatever reason, Irish-Aer Lingus has proved highly popular with the flying public: on the intensely competitive trans-Atlantic route it has very often ranked tops among all airlines in the percentage of seats filled.

WHAT TO TAKE

As Ireland is an island, sudden rainshowers come up from the Atlantic frequently—showers usually are brief, but they can be hard, and may occur several times a day. Take along rubber boots (those that fit over shoes and fold up are convenient) if you are going to do any exploration of the countryside, as you will be crossing a lot of wet pastures. An umbrella will also be useful.

Women can feel free to wear pants (Irishwomen do), and you will be glad you did when it comes to climbing those picturesque stone walls Ireland is famous for. In general, take informal clothes.

Take a warm sweater—even if you plan to buy one of the hand-knit Aran sweaters that are such bargains in Ireland.

Most visitors stay in government-recommended guest houses where accommodations are reasonable and comfortable, but where you will have to bring your own wash cloth if you want one. Another good item, especially if you will be traveling a lot, is a bar of your favorite soap. Guest houses usually provide soap; but roadside stop points may not. You may also want to take your own tissues or toilet paper as the Irish variety tends to be rough.

Laundry and dry-cleaning present no problem in Irish cities, where commercial establishments can process clothes within hours. These services are, however, expensive, so budget travelers are advised to bring at least some drip-dry clothes.

If you intend to ride, hunt, golf or fish you should obviously bring the appropriate gear. For hiking, a pair of good stout shoes is a must. As for beachwear, forget it: the Irish and visiting Britishers disporting themselves by the sea may be having a high old time, but the water is too cold and the air too cool for most of us sun-spoiled North Americans. If you belatedly discover a strain of Eskimo blood in your veins you can always buy a swim suit on the spot.

TIPS FOR PHOTOGRAPHERS

Ireland, with its varied scenery and abundance of picturesque views, is one of the most photogenic countries on earth. It can also be one of the most frustrating for photographers: no sooner are you ready to snap a colorful scene than the sun goes behind a cloud. For color photographs always use a haze filter, as there's always some haze on the landscape even when the sun is shining brightly. Kodachrome-X or high-speed Ektachrome are fine for Ireland. Black-and-white film can be developed and printed just about anywhere. In Dublin you should have no difficulty finding places that will process color and/or motion picture film.

CUSTOMS

Irish customs officials are courteous, efficient and quick. After checking your passport they will probably ask you, very politely,

The dying craft of thatching, Co. Wicklow

to open your bags for inspection. You are allowed to bring in all ordinary personal effects duty-free, and there is no limit to the amount of dollars and/or travelers' cheques you may bring in. Visitors from the U.S. and Canada can bring in a thousand cigarettes (five cartons) duty-free, or 200 cigars, or 2½ pounds of tobacco; since tobacco is costly in Ireland, smokers are well advised to pack their necessaries. One quart of liquor and two bottles of wine can be brought in without payment of duty, as can one pint of perfume. Goods intended as gifts for Irish friends can be brought in to the value of $24 for each adult in a party and $10 for each child (tobacco and spirits may not be brought in by travelers under 15). Contraband items, which will be confiscated, include narcotics, contraceptives, obscene books, feathers, pig meat and unlicensed firearms.

CURRENCY

American or Canadian bills (but not coins) are accepted in most Irish establishments, provided their denominations are not too high. Since your change will be in Irish or British currency you might just as well simplify matters by exchanging your dollars for the local specie at the earliest opportunity. This can be done with a minimum of fuss at any bank, or at the larger hotels.

Irish currency presents no difficulties to travelers who have mastered British money; Irish bills and coins have the same value as their British equivalents and even bear the same names. The two currencies are interchangeable, and both circulate throughout the Irish Republic and Northern Ireland. (Irish currency is not, however, accepted in Britain except in banks—a point to be kept in mind by travelers proceeding to England, Scotland or Wales.)

The basic unit of the Irish currency is the pound (symbol: £); in February of 1971, Irish currency went over to the decimal system, and the pound is now divided into one hundred new pence (symbol p.), each equivalent to 2 United States cents. (For practical purposes, consider that the pence is worth 2 cents, and the pound worth about $2.07. The denominations, distinguishing symbols, and value in American currency are given in the following chart. When giving American equivalencies for specific prices, elsewhere in the guide, the prices are rounded off to the nearest cent.

Denomination		Symbol	Value
50	pence	Woodcock	$1.00
10	pence	Salmon	20 cents
5	pence	Bull	10 cents
2	pence	Adaptation of ornamental bird detail	4 cents
1	penny	Adaptation of ornamental bird detail	2 cents
½	penny	Adaptation of ornamental bird detail	1 cent

Many people still think in the old shillings, but almost all prices are quoted in new pence. They occasionally forget and ask you for "ten bob" (ten shillings or fifty new pence), but they are always quick to translate into the new system when they notice your quizzical expression. The conversion is quite simple. One shilling is the same as five new pence. There are twenty shillings in a pound and twenty-one in a guinea (which hardly exists any more except in the most snobbish shops).

Irish banknotes are issued in six denominations:

£	1 (a quid)	$ 2
£	5 (a fiver)	$ 10
£	10	$ 20
£	20	$ 40
£	50	$100
£	100	$200

GETTING AROUND IN IRELAND

Ireland is blissfully easy to get around in. For one thing, the country has 52,000 miles of good, paved roads—about six times the ratio of roadage to people in neighboring Britain. For another, only one citizen in six owns a car. So if you drive, the roads are all yours—apart from an occasional bus, tractor, wagon or cart. The traffic you encounter will mostly be pedestrians—an old farm woman in a black shawl, a boy carrying a load of sun-dried peat, or a flock of sheep being herded to market by a sheepdog and her master. Being so free of traffic, the roads of Ireland are ideal for hiking and bicycling.

Ireland's relative lack of cars also has an advantage for travelers who prefer to get around by public transport, since it means that the government has to maintain a network of railway and bus lines extensive enough to serve the entire country.

Getting around in the cities. The top deck, or "upper saloon" of a double-decker bus (where smoking is permitted) offers a fine vantage point from which to view an Irish city, while listening in on the lilting talk around you. But unless you know your way about you may find yourself a long way from where you want to go by the time the conductor comes by to collect your fare—and informs you, when you tell him your destination, that you're on the wrong bus. (True, he and/or your fellow passengers will immediately set you straight, but getting to where you're going may, by then, require one or more changes of bus.) The city buses of Ireland rarely proceed along one thoroughfare for long but wind this way and that among a maze of streets. Dublin has no less than eighty different bus routes, and Cork fourteen.

If you have an appointment in town or want to visit some place that is not within walking distance, your best move is to take a taxi. Anyone can direct you to the nearest taxi rank. Away from the city center you can summon a taxi by telephone (under "Taxis" in the directory). One suggestion: if you see a taxi going past don't hail it until you're sure it isn't a police car —although the policemen (called by their Gaelic name *gardai*) would not be offended.

Most Irish cities are small; even central, non-residential Dublin is not too large to be covered on foot. When it comes to savoring the atmosphere of an Irish city there just is no better way of going about it.

Around Ireland by public transport. Except for a few very small local bus lines, all trains and buses in the Republic are run by the government's *Coras Iompair Eireann* (Irish Transport System), commonly called C.I.E. From its headquarters at Heuston Station in Dublin C.I.E. operates local buses, provincial (long distance) buses, known as coaches, and 1650 miles of railway service, together with a number of sightseeing tours and regular boat sailings between Galway and the Aran Islands. Timetables for all trains and provincial buses in the country can be obtained at any train or bus station. For all passenger inquiries the number to call is 787777 in Dublin.

C.I.E. provides considerable travel bargains in the form of "Rambler tickets", good for 8 or 15 days of unlimited travel throughout the Republic. A standard rail travel ticket costs $27 (8 days) or $39 (15 days), and one for both rail and provincial bus travel $34 (8 days) or $48 (15 days). A ticket called the "Overlander", available from April through September, provides you with unlimited rail and bus travel for 8 or 15 days in both the Republic and Northern Ireland—all for $48 (8 days) or $60 (15 days). For a couple with at least one child, reductions are available on "Rambler" tickets. Children under 16 are entitled to half-fare "Rambler" tickets and children under 15 to half-fare "Overlanders".

By train. Irish trains are roomy and comfortable with huge windows. Most include a buffet car, if not a restaurant car. Meals on the trains are good and, by American standards, very reasonable. The service charge and taxes are automatically included in the price.

One mystery concerning the C.I.E. trains defies explanation. Of all the alien forces who have set foot in Ireland few have been disliked more than the British mercenary soldiers—the notorious "black and tans". Yet today, every railway car in Ireland is painted in those very colors—why, no one can say.

By provincial bus. The provincial buses, mostly red single-deckers with scrolls up front announcing such mysterious destinations as CORCAIGH (Cork) and LUIMNEACH (Limerick), are less comfortable than the trains. But instead of streaking along between stations situated on the fringes of towns and cities, they proceed at a slower pace through Ireland's agricultural heartland, stopping at the very centers of towns, villages and hamlets. In doing so they enable a visitor to get closer to the Irish countryside—and especially to the Irish country people, who, having no cars, use the buses to get to school or to work, to market or to mass, or just to visit a friend a few miles down the road.

Any visitor taking his first bus ride through rural Ireland could conclude that the operation was not only haphazard but a little mad. Again and again the bus halts to take on a passenger at some solitary spot which could not possibly be a regular stop. At every village and town on the route the conductor delivers a fistful of mysterious cylinders, wrapped in brown paper, to the local grocery, general store, or candy store. And at the rest stops, which seem to occur at least three times every hour, both driver and conductor disappear into a pub on the town square, to emerge several minutes later wearing satisfied expressions and wiping their mouths with the backs of their hands. Yet when the bus arrives at his destination, the visitor finds, on consulting his watch, that the time is precisely that given in his timetable.

Eventually, the "mysteries" are cleared up. Irish buses do indeed stop anywhere, at any time, for anybody. The brown-wrapped cylinders are simply newspapers, for buses do double duty as mail carriers. And the frequent rest stops are a practical necessity if a person indulges now and then in the Irish national tipple, stout.

By car. Although the trains and (especially) the provincial buses afford fine opportunities for seeing the country while observing the people close up, both methods of transport oblige the visitor to travel by specific routes, at specific times. (On Sundays, both services operate on a restricted basis.) A visitor who wants to see as much as possible of the country in a limited time can do so best by making his way around Ireland by car.

Apart from the expense of shipping your car across the Atlantic, there are several other compelling reasons for leaving it at home. Gas (called petrol) is expensive in Ireland, costing $1.60 a gallon or more. The Irish roads are narrower than ours, having been built to handle smaller vehicles than our behemoths.

Finally, in Ireland you drive on the *left*.

By renting a small car, which costs less than a big one, and uses less gas, you can cover the whole country at remarkably little expense—and enjoy the pleasure of driving through mile after mile of heartbreakingly beautiful country without billboards, hot dog stands, or traffic jams.

If you can only spare a few days to visit Ireland, pick up a car at one of the two airports, drive it along some scenic routes on the south coast, and drop it off at the other airport. If Ireland is the first country on your European itinerary you could drive from Shannon Airport to Dublin; if the last, you could drive the other way, turning in your rented car at Shannon before winging your way home.

Self-drive cars for hire. To hire a car in Ireland you must be over 21 and under 70 (or, for some car rental firms, between 23 and 65) and in possession of a current national driver's license or an International Driver's Permit. If you take out the optional insurance (£1 a day, or £6.50 a week) you probably won't be asked for a deposit; if you don't, you will be asked for a returnable deposit of £10 or £15 depending on the car.

Car-hire rates vary, of course, with the type of car you rent and with the season. In the fall, winter, and spring you can rent a small car (e.g. a Fiat 850) for about £24 per week or £5 per day, all mileage included. In the high season—July, August, September and the Christmas and Easter holidays—the standard weekly charge for the same car is about £36 weekly, £7 daily, all mileage included. Gas costs about $1.60 per gallon.

There are several reliable firms which have desks at all three airports, and thus lend themselves to the one-way tour of the south coast mentioned. Some of these are:

Avis Rent-a-Car, 1 Hanover Street East, Dublin (Tel. 776971).

Johnson & Perrott, 12a South Leinster Street, Dublin (Tel. 767213).

Cahills, 36 Annesley Place, Dublin (Tel. 747766).

Murrays Pal Rent-a-Car, Baggot Street Bridge, Dublin (Tel. 763221).

Hertz Rent-a-Car, Hume House, Ballsbridge, Dublin (684711).

Dan Ryan Rent-a-Car, 42 Parkgate Street, Dublin (Tel. 776631).

Most of the above have offices in other major cities of Ireland.

Good road maps covering the whole of Ireland can be obtained at Texaco or Esso service stations for about 15 pence (30¢). In the U.S. or Canada, the Irish Tourist Board will furnish you with a free road map which has the most scenic routes

A familiar Dublin landmark—the Customs House

outlined in green. Ireland's Ordnance Survey Board issues a series of twenty-five maps covering every part of the country in detail; they cost about $1 each. The Board, and a firm called Geographia, also put out large maps of the island which can be bought in bookstores and stationery shops for 37 pence (about 75 cents).

By horse-drawn caravan. This delightful mode of transport, a survivor from the leisurely days before the automobile, may be just the answer for a family of three or four, or for two compatible couples traveling together. What you get is a compact, barrel-shaped enclosed vehicle containing beds or bunks, kitchenware, a small gas stove and lamps—and a gentle horse to pull it. You need no experience of handling a horse, just the common sense to feed it the oats which the company supplies, or let it graze. Rental of a caravan and horse comes to between £15 and £46 a week, depending on the location and the season.

You must write a company directly to reserve a caravan, enclosing at least a quarter of the fee as a deposit. In July and August all available caravans are usually booked, so it's a good idea to write well in advance. Some caravan companies in scenic areas are:

Blarney Romany Caravans, Lancaster House, Western Road, Cork.

West Cork Caravan Co., 27 Rossa Street, Clonakilty, County Cork.

David Slattery Caravans, 1 Russell Street, Tralee, County Kerry.

Shannon Horse Caravans, Adare, County Limerick.

Lough Gill Caravans Ltd., Drumlease Glebe House, Droma-hair, County Leitrim.

Connemara Horse Caravans, Westport, County Mayo.

Gipsy Rover Caravans, Tudor Lodge, Church Road, Bally-brack, County Roscommon.

Bray Caravan Company, Main Street, Bray, County Wicklow.

By bicycle. Bicycles can be rented in Ireland for very little. Even in Dublin the charges are absurdly low by American standards: £1 a day, £4.75 (about $9.50) a week, with a deposit of £3. Raleigh Rent-a-Bike has a network throughout the country.

Sightseeing tours. All sightseeing tours in Ireland are run by C.I.E. and start from about twenty centers. Itineraries, time-tables and prices are listed in illustrated folders, entitled *Day Trips;* at all C.I.E. depots and tourist offices.

Scenic drives and city tours average about 2½ hours and cost 85 pence. Seven-hour tours begin at £1.80, while all-day tours lasting more than twelve hours begin at £2.50. On all tours children under fifteen pay half fare.

THE IRISH LANGUAGE

Only a century and a quarter ago most Irish people spoke the ancient Gaelic tongue (in a form now called Irish to distinguish it from the Scottish and Welsh varieties). Irish then gave ground to English, until, at the close of the century, only a few thousand people spoke it—most of them peasant farmers and fisherfolk in remote parts of the west. At about that time, a group of young intellectuals, including the poet Yeats, began to be interested in the vast body of Celtic folklore and literature written in Gaelic. This cultural movement soon acquired a political cast as the leaders of the independence movement came to recognize its potential for fostering pride in the national heritage. When Ireland became free, Irish was officially made one of the two national languages. Ever since, all school children have been taught Irish; until recently, a knowledge of the language was a prerequisite for a career in the civil service; and all public signs have been printed in Irish alongside the English equivalent. Successive Irish governments have promoted the use of Irish as a fixed national policy.

In spite of the earnest efforts of government and private groups, the campaign to restore Irish as a living language has not met with success. Census estimates claim a quarter of the Republic's citizens are Irish-speakers, but less than 30,000 Irish people, one per cent of the population, actually use Irish as their everyday language. And of these, all but a fraction speak English as well!

With regard to the signs in Irish that confront him at every turn, the visitor may be momentarily baffled by some *Seomra Feithimh* for Waiting Room, *Deochlann* for Lounge Bar). But he may also be amused by the heroic efforts exerted to make Irish conform to the modern world (as in *Ard Musaeum* for Art Museum, *Traein* for Trains, and *Telefon* for Telephone). The Irish words a visitor might need to know are the ones over the doors of public toilets: *Mna* for Women and *Fir* for Men. One word he might hear spoken, and can learn himself, is *slainte* (pronounced "slawń-cheh"), a salutation given over a brimming glass of Guinness, equal to "good luck", "here's to you", "bottoms up", etc., etc.

One curious fact about Irish is that it lacks equivalents of "yes" and "no". This is presumably why the Irish tend to avoid these English monosyllables in response to a yes-or-no question, preferring to answer instead, "I did", "I did not", "I will", "I will not", or whatever.

WHERE TO STAY

Accommodations in Ireland fall into three main categories. First, there are hotels, which serve three meals a day and are licensed to sell alcoholic beverages. Second, there are the guesthouses, smaller, cheaper, and less formal than the hotels, but clean and comfortable. Guesthouses always serve breakfast (often referred to as "bed and breakfast" houses) and often serve teas as well; they do not sell liquor. Last, but distinctly not least, are the farmhouses and private homes whose owners have a few rooms to let; besides costing very little, these places often provide pleasant, cozy accommodation.

The Irish Tourist Board lists all accommodations in the country, which have met its approval, in two publications: *Official Guide to Hotels and Guesthouses*, and *Town and Country Homes, Farmhouses, Hostels in Ireland*, both costing 15 pence (35 cents). *Farm Holidays in Ireland* is the official publication of the Irish Farm Holidays Association. Proprietors of listed accomodations are not allowed to charge higher prices than published.

There are half a dozen top-rank hotels in Dublin, one or two in Cork, and one at Shannon Airport. Elsewhere, hotels tend to be more modest. Notable exceptions are the gracious, old-fashioned and commodious establishments of the Great Southern

Hotel chain—one each in Sligo, Galway and Killarney, with others at Kenmare and Parknasilla in County Kerry, Mulrany in County Mayo and Bundoran in County Donegal.

Generally speaking, the traveler gets most for his money in guesthouses, where his bed-and-breakfast may come to £2 ($4.00) or less. Incidentally, the price of *all* accommodations, except in a few luxury hotels, includes breakfast. And in Ireland that means a very hearty repast; fruit juice, toast or rolls, hot or cold cereal, bacon and eggs, sausages and eggs, or finnan haddie (fish) all washed down with an enormous pot of tea.

Information on selected accommodations at various locations is given in the Fact Finder at the end of this book.

EATING IN IRELAND

Ireland is hardly a gastronomical paradise, but food there is plentiful and good. And the people eat well: year after year, surveys conducted under United Nations auspices show that their per capita intake of calories exceeds that of any other nation in the world.

Cooking will never challenge conversation as a popular pastime in Ireland, but Irish cooks know what they're doing, and most of the foods they use come straight from nearby natural sources. Tender lamb and beef fattened on lush limestone grass, fresh chickens and eggs, trout and salmon from the lakes and rivers, plus the world-renowned Dublin Bay prawns and Galway oysters. So you can be sure that your meals in Ireland will be tasty and nourishing.

Irish cuisine features a few native dishes. Spicy, delicious soups, among the most satisfying anywhere; coarse-textured Irish soda bread is delicious, and the famous Irish stew. There are too a number of local specialties concocted with the innards and/or blood of farm animals, such as black tripe (Counties Wexford and Waterford), tripe and drisheen (County Cork) and blood pudding (around Limerick); but some visitors feel a bit squeamish about these. Also there is a dessert called carrageen, made from a kind of seaweed and flavored with lemon.

What you may miss is that lavish combination of imagination and pain which turns a meal into an event. If you insist on a high gastronomic standard there are a small number of first-rate restaurants in Dublin and a few elsewhere, but the cooking will be French and the check sizeable.

As a society based on agriculture the Irish naturally conform in their eating habits to the pattern of farm life. The first meal of the day is a hearty breakfast, the mid-day meal a substantial dinner and the evening meal either high tea or a relatively light supper. You can, of course, have dinner in the evening if you prefer, but you will undoubtedly have to pay a good deal more than you would for the same dishes at mid-day. In Dublin you can get a snack up until 4 A.M., and in most towns until 11:30 or midnight.

The cheapest complete meals you can get in Ireland are served in simple establishments which, as in England, are called cafés. Regular restaurants range from the inexpensive places that cater to students to the expensive French variety. Chinese and Indian restaurants, when you find them, are very modestly priced and have a wide selection of dishes. Most pubs serve light snacks at lunch time, and sandwiches or potato chips (called "crisps") are available at other hours. What the Irish call a sandwich, by the way, we would consider half a sandwich; in Ireland a complete sandwich—that is, both halves—is called a "round".

DRINKING IN IRELAND

A "round" means something else, too, in Irish pubs: namely, the round of drinks a man stands his companions and himself. The drinks could be any kind, but eight times out of ten, in any place, time or season they will be Guinness. Manufactured in a vast Dublin brewery (but not, as legend has it, from the brownish waters of the River Liffey), Guinness is a rich, full-bodied stout, dark brown in color, with a creamy white head. Americans, accustomed to the light, clear brew which Irishmen call lager, may have to acquire a taste for the stuff, but when they do there is no weaning them. The Irish can be quite fanatical about the virtues of Guinness; though the greatest skeptics on earth, they accept at face value the brewers' claim that "Guinness is good for you". Doctors regularly prescribe it for convalescents, and even teetotalers (of whom there are a surprising number in Ireland) have been known to take it for their health.

If you have never sampled Irish whiskey, you certainly ought to. Its flavor, very different from that of Scotch, evokes the aroma of peat smoke rising from fires under the distilling vats. Irishmen usually drink it neat, but many visitors prefer to take it with coffee, sugar and lightly whipped cream—Irish coffee.

Ireland produces its own gin, too, which, like the native whiskey, costs less than imported varieties.

Most Irish pubs are family-run affairs. In the Republic they are open weekdays from 10:30 A.M. to 11:00 P.M. in the winter, and until 11:30 P.M. in the summer. In Dublin and Cork, the pubs shut their doors on weekday afternoons between 2:30 and 3:30; this pause is irreverently known as the "holy hour". In Northern Ireland, the pubs do business from 10 in the morning

"Bare ruined choirs"— Ardfert Cathedral, Co. Kerry

to 11 at night on weekdays and are closed all day Sundays, as in Scotland.

Bar prices are fairly uniform in the Republic: a pint of Guinness generally costs 26 pence in Dublin, and 24 pence elsewhere. Spirits come higher, but are still cheap by Stateside standards: a "small" whiskey, containing more liquor than most American bar jiggers, is about 30 pence. Prices tend to be a penny or two higher in Northern Ireland.

In Ireland there are a handful of establishments that could be called nightclubs—and then only by stretching the imagination. For Irishmen of all classes the pub is the natural center of social life, especially after dark. Irish pubs vary greatly. In Dublin they range from ornate Edwardian places with crystal chandeliers, oak and mahogany paneling, cut-glass mirrors and often double as general stores and the congregating-place of the local populace. In sophisticated Dublin, by contrast, different pubs cater to distinct clienteles: in one the regulars will mostly be students, in another journalists, in a third theatre people, and so on.

A distinct Irish drinking place, which no visitor should miss, is the singing pub or ballad club. There are several excellent establishments of this kind in the Dublin area, notably the celebrated Abbey Tavern at Howth, and one in Galway. At the best of these places you pay a modest entrance fee of 50 pence ($1.00) for an evening of vigorous and varied musical entertainment while you quaff away. The songs run the gamut from sentimental favorites to rollicking country tunes to rousing patriotic ballads, and are rendered by melodious Irish voices to the music of a piano, fiddle, guitar, banjo, harp, or combination thereof.

A few pubs remain exclusively male hangouts, and women (especially those without male escorts) will be met by unfriendly stares, and a crowd with no other women in it. In such pubs—and they are becoming ever fewer—beat a hasty retreat. Ladies are entirely welcome, however, in the lounge bars or the "snugs" adjoining all but the meanest pubs—normally upstairs or in the rear, with the way clearly marked. And they can, of course, feel perfectly easy about drinking in restaurants and hotel bars.

TIPPING

In Ireland, the tipping problem is not (yet) an insidious nuisance. Most hotels and guesthouses include a service charge in your bill, and many restaurants do the same. Normally, the only person you would tip at your hotel would be the porter who takes your bags to your room. Unless you are traveling in tremendous style, 15 to 20 pence (30 to 40 cents) should be plenty.

Taxi drivers expect a modest tip—say, fifteen per cent of the fare. As for a hired driver or guide, there is no hard and fast rule; the amount you give him above and beyond his fee is up to you. Often, in circumstances which would seem to call for a tip, your proffered coins will be politely refused—not out of pride, but simply because the natural courtesy of the Irish toward strangers militates against their taking money for a friendly, helpful act.

SHOPPING

There are some really terrific bargains to be found in Ireland, particularly handcrafts. The United States government won't let you bring home more than a hundred dollars' worth duty free, but most Irish goods are still bargains even if you have to pay duty on them of between 10% and 20% of their value. And there's no limit to the number of parcels you can send home, provided the contents of each is valued at $10 or less and you send no more than one a day to the same address. Cautionary note: on your hundred-dollar duty-free allowance you can only import one quart of liquor.

The best buys in Ireland are: hand-woven tweeds and woolens, hand-knit sweaters; linen; lace; and Waterford crystal and glass. Your fancy might also be struck by: jewelry made from Connemara marble, a sheep-skin coat, a copy of the 1916 Proclamation (the Irish Declaration of Independence). Excellent bargains in old books and antique silver are to be found in Dublin. In the line of meaningful souvenirs, you might want to buy a Claddagh ring; embodying a traditional design of two hands holding a crowned heart, this unique ring was exchanged in marriage centuries ago by fisherfolk in the Claddagh district of Galway, and is now given and received as a token of love.

Naturally, all Irish goods are least expensive at the source: the weaver's or knitter's cottage, the workshop or the factory. But in compact Ireland distribution presents few problems and the retailer's overhead is relatively low; consequently the markup on most items is modest. On some lines, such as Waterford crystal, prices are fixed throughout the Republic. So there is really no need to hunt around for bargains, though the department stores in the cities can usually offer goods at slightly lower prices than the smaller specialty shops.

Irish linen, a product of Northern Ireland, is known and prized around the world. Gossamer Carrickmacross lace is made in County Monaghan, while Limerick lace comes, of course, from the famous old port at the mouth of the Shannon. Irish tweeds are woven in the west, and specifically in the highlands of County Donegal, in the extreme northwest of the Republic. Waterford crystal and glass, esteemed everywhere for the fine workmanship

Trinity College, Dublin, breeder of great men

that goes into their shaping and into the carving of their traditional designs, are fashioned by hand in the sturdy old seaport of
Waterford, in the southeast. The incomparable Aran sweaters
are so called because they are part of the traditional garb of
fishermen on the rugged Aran Islands, far out in Galway Bay;
they are also called *bainin* sweaters (pronounced "baw-neen")
for their natural wool which is a cream-colored and lightly
coated in animal oils which makes them water-repellent. Connemara marble jewelry is fashioned from the green stone quarried
in Ireland's "wild west."

Just to save shopping time you might want to know (if you
don't already) that Grafton Street is the Bond Street/Fifth
Avenue of Dublin. In Cork, the equivalent thoroughfare is Patrick Street; in Limerick, O'Connell Street; in Galway, Shop
Street. In Londonderry you might start at The Diamond and
investigate the shops on the streets leading away from it, while
in Belfast you can easily find what you want on Donegall Square
and on adjacent Donegall Place and College Street.

No visitor interested in contemporary arts and crafts should
miss the Kilkenny Design Center. Kilkenny, 75 miles southwest
of Dublin, is an exceptionally pretty little city, even for Ireland.
It has a magnificent old cathedral and an imposing medieval
castle which was, until very recently, a seat of the Butler family
—earls (now marquesses) of Ormonde. The former stables and
grooms' quarters adjacent to the castle now house the workshops
of designers in many fields and from many lands, notably Scandi-
navia, Britain and Germany. At the Irish government's expense,
these talented men and women are creating modern production
models which employ traditional Irish designs, and meanwhile
training young Irish craftsmen and artists. On display in the
spacious showroom are stunning examples of silver and iron-
ware, ceramics, woven goods, textile prints, and turned wood.

Unless you are traveling around the country by car, you may
be reluctant to load up with many purchases. The duty-free shop
at the Shannon Free International Airport (where westbound
planes from Dublin stop for about three quarters of an hour)
offers a solution. In the shop you will find all sorts of Irish goods
plus items like perfume from other European lands, selling for as
little as half the U.S. or Canadian price. Picking up his purchases
at Shannon, the visitor can check them through with his other
baggage and never give them a second thought until he arrives
at his New World destination.

ACTIVE SPORTS

Didn't Stanyhurst call the Irish "excellent horsemen"? And didn't
Mr. Yeats's committee decide, three and a half centuries later,

that a horse should adorn Ireland's highest-value coin, the half crown? He did and it did. For the Irish esteem horses above all other creatures.

Naturally, horses are available for *riding* just about everywhere —at an average hourly charge of about £2 ($4). *Pony-trekking* is increasingly popular—this being an escorted ride through the countryside during which participants stop to view historical ruins and have lunch. A pony-trek lasting all day may cost about £7 (about $14), with lunch extra. Organized pony-treks exist in all the more scenic areas of the island, such as County Wicklow, County Kerry, the Killaloe region at the foot of Lough Derg and the foothills of the Mountains of Mourne, in Northern Ireland's County Down.

Hunting is a favorite Irish sport, and more than eighty packs of hounds are maintained on the island. Visitors are welcome to hunt with a few packs: the Bray Harriers, the Fingal Harriers, the South County Dublin Foxhounds and the Ward Union.

Golf may have originated in Scotland, but Ireland probably has more golf courses per capita than any country in the world. There are 240 in all, more than 200 in the Republic and the rest in Northern Ireland. 103 of these have eighteen holes, including twenty or more courses of championship class. Such seaside links as Portmarnock near Dublin and Waterville in County Kerry are rated among the world's best. Yet greens fees average out at somewhere around £2 ($4) for an entire day of golfing!

A list of Irish golf club facilities available to visitors is obtainable from travel agents or any Irish tourist office.

Tennis enthusiasts can indulge in their favorite pastime for as little as 40 pence ($1) a day. A number of seaside tennis clubs rent courts to the public, and Dublin has some municipal courts as well.

Fishing. With its myriad clear streams, rivers and lakes, Ireland is one of the greatest countries for this sport. In most places fishing is free. The Irish angler's favorite diversions are brown trout fishing and coarse fishing (for pike, perch, bream, etc.); no license is needed for either. Fishing for salmon or sea trout does require a license, which costs £1 for a week, £3 for three weeks and £4 for a year, and is good throughout the Republic. Some of the best salmon fisheries are preserved, but a visitor can buy tickets to fish them at rates ranging from 50 pence ($1.00) to ten pounds ($20.00) a week. But salmon fishing is good—and costs nothing—on many lovely stretches of water, including the fabled

Lakes of Killarney, Lough Corrib near Galway, Lough Conn and Lough Gern.

Thanks to the Gulf Stream, which washes its southern and western coasts, Ireland is also a paradise for deep-sea anglers. The coastal waters teem with a remarkable variety of fish, from mackerel to shark. Off-shore fishing is free, but you will have to pay for the motor launch—usually about £3.50 per person per day. The chief center for sea-fishing on Ireland's south coast is Kinsale, in County Cork.

Fishing tackle can be readily bought or rented in Ireland.

The Irish Tourist Board maintains an Anglers' Information Service at 63/67 Stephen Street, Dublin 2 (telephone 765871), which provides expert advice on all fishing matters.

Fishermen and curragh—Aran Islands, Co. Galway

Speaking of water sports, these three may interest the visitor: Boats can be rented for *sailing* at sailing clubs around the coast. *Water-skiing* is increasingly popular on rivers, lakes and bays. And *boating* along the lordly, uncrowded Shannon, while hardly qualifying as a sport, is a marvelous way to spend a week. Details on all these activities can be obtained from the Irish Tourist Board.

SPECTATOR SPORTS

As you might expect, *horse racing* is very big in Ireland. Races are scheduled throughout the year at the three Dublin tracks.

The big national events are all held at the Curragh in County Kildare, where the Irish Sweepstakes Derby is run in late June or early July for stakes of £100,000 (almost a quarter of a million dollars). Regular meetings are held at race courses throughout the country, and racing festivals lasting two days or more are held at Bellewstown, Fairyhouse, Galway, Killarney, Listowel, Punchestown, Tralee and Tramore. Consult the Irish Tourist Board's *Calendar of Events* for dates.

Greyhound racing is also popular in Ireland. Races are held six nights a week in Dublin and somewhat less frequently at tracks in smaller cities.

Ireland's two great national sports which involve men rather than animals are *hurling* and *Gaelic football*. Both have fifteen men on a side. Hurling is a fast-paced game, something like field hockey, in which players equipped with sticks, called hurleys, strive to project a small, hard ball into their opponents' goal. Gaelic football is much like soccer (which is, of course, called football outside the United States). In the case of both sports, the All-Ireland championship finals, between the two top-ranking county teams, are played in September in Dublin's outdoor stadium, Croke Park.

DIVERSIONS

Glories of Irish drama and Irish acting are too well known to require comment here, and the pleasures of playgoing in Dublin —summed up in the magic words "The Abbey"—are almost as familiar.

What may not be so well known is that after a run in the capital the original company often takes a show on tour, playing theatres in the larger provincial towns. Thus a person visiting, say, Connemara might easily discover that a play he has wanted to see is being staged by the Dublin company in Galway. Ticket prices in Ireland are anything but off-putting: they range from 50 pence for a local group's production, to £2 for a sample of the finest theatre in the English language—at the Abbey or Gate Theatres in Dublin.

Every Irish town of any size has at least one cinema (movie house). Seats cost from 50 pence to £1.

The shows known as cabarets put on in hotel ballrooms or theatres can be fun—*clean* fun, for the Irish are rather prudish in such matters. Akin to cabaret are the "Irish Nights" staged in the larger hotels and pubs. At an Irish Night the entertainment is exclusively native. The master of ceremonies is invariably an Irish comedian with a repertoire of Irish jokes, and a typical bill would comprise a soprano soloist, a ballad-belting male quartet, a lady harpist-singer and a trio of little girls, in traditional costume, who demonstrate Irish dance steps. Admission is usually free in pubs, but at hotels (where the program is probably relatively sophisticated) it may be as much as 75 pence.

The Irish adore dancing, and wherever you may be in Ireland on a Saturday evening there is sure to be a nearby dance open to the public. In the country, admission will probably be no more than 5 pence (10 cents), and the music will mostly be jigs and reels. A country dance is well worth going to, if only to take in the wondrously fast fiddling and the dancers' fancy footwork. With the aid of a pint or two you might even work up the courage to have a fling yourself.

Dances begin at 9 P.M., but they don't really get going until around 11, when the pubs close. After the dance ends, at 1 A.M., nightowls in Dublin can still linger over coffee or tea and snacks in any of several cafés until they, too, close down at 4, by which time anyone should be ready to hit the hay.

FESTIVALS AND SPECIAL EVENTS

Every year a number of festivals and special events occur at various places in Ireland. They are friendly, easygoing affairs, at which the local people mix happily with visitors. Prices are well within the means of the most modest traveler. For the location and dates of all festivals and special events, including sports fixtures, horse races and concerts, you should consult the Irish Tourist Board's leaflet *Calendar of Events* for the upcoming year.

A short list of Ireland's major festivals and special events would include:

May. The Dundalk Maytime Festival (County Louth); the International Choral and Folk Dance Festival (Cork); the Kilkenny Beer Festival (County Kilkenny); the Spring Show, a national livestock fair held in the Ballsbridge section of Dublin; and Pan Celtic Week (Killarney, County Kerry).

June. The International Deep Sea Angling Festival (Westport, County Mayo); and the Irish Sweeps Derby (sometimes run early in July), at the Curragh, County Kildare. The Cork Film International; Festival in Great Irish Houses; and the Donegal International Car Rally.

July. Mary from Dunloe Festival (County Kerry); Bach Festival (Killarney, County Kerry); and the Galway Races.

August. The Dublin Horse Show, Ireland's great annual social event (Ballsbridge, Dublin); Irish Antique Dealers Fair (Dublin); *Fleadh Cheoil na hEireann* (a gathering of traditional Irish musicians); and the Yeats Summer School, held in Sligo.

September. The Festival of Kerry (Tralee, County Kerry); the

Pony-trekking near Killaloe, Co. Clare

Festival of Light Opera (Waterford); the Puck Fair (County Kerry); All-Ireland Hurling and Football Finals, (Dublin); and the Oyster Festival of Galway.

October. *An tOireachtas,* a national Celtic cultural event (Dublin); Dublin Theatre Festival; Castlebar International Song Contest (County Mayo), and the Festival of Opera (Wexford).

TRACING IRISH ANCESTORS

The Office of the Registrar-General in the Custom House, Dublin, contains birth and death records for all Ireland from 1864 to the present, and records of non-Catholic marriages since 1845. Records which pertain to the six counties of Northern Ireland are in Belfast, at the Office of the Registrar-General on Ormeau Avenue. The Public Record Office in the Four Courts, Dublin, contains data on land-ownership in the early nineteenth century. Other useful sources of information in Dublin are the Registry of Deeds on Henrietta Street (deeds dating back to 1708); the National Library on Kildare Street (a vast assemblage of Hiberniana); and the Genealogical Office of the National Library in Dublin Castle (genealogies and heraldic data back to the seventeenth century).

The Superintendent Registrar's Office in each of the county capitals contains duplicate records for the county. The parish records of Catholic churches throughout the island have records of christenings. Information about Presbyterian ancestors may be found at the Presbyterian Historical Society in Church House, Fisherwick Place, Belfast. Additional comprehensive records dealing with Northern Ireland are at the Public Record Office of Northern Ireland, the Law Courts Building, May Street.

Once you have dug up a firm clue as to when and where a particular ancestor lived, you might visit the place and talk to a few of the older inhabitants. They might well be able to provide additional information, for in Ireland memories are long, going back far beyond the lifetime of a mere individual.

MEETING THE IRISH

The Irish are not, heaven knows, hard to meet. But if your time is limited and you would like to get acquainted with an Irish person in your profession or business or with whom you share some other common interest a meeting can easily be arranged through the *Meet the Irish Program* sponsored by the Irish Tourist Board. To do so, you should write the Board at Baggot Street Bridge, Dublin, well in advance of your trip to request a "Meet the Irish" form. Fill it out and return it at least a month before your trip. Before you leave for Ireland you will receive particulars as to whom you will meet where.

HOLIDAYS

Throughout Ireland, the principal holidays are those common to all Christian countries—Christmas and Easter, together with New Year's Day. But most other important holidays are only celebrated on one side of the border. The Republic's annual occasion for patriotic display is, naturally, March 17, St. Patrick's Day. In Northern Ireland the equivalent day for Protestants is July 12, the anniversary of King William's victory over King James at the Battle of the Boyne. The Republic likewise observes the major feast days of the Catholic calendar, such as Assumption Day (August 15), while Northern Ireland (except for the Catholic minority) does not.

Sunday is a day of worship and rest throughout Ireland. The people of Northern Ireland, with their predominantly Scots-Presbyterian background and outlook, keep the Sabbath with particular rigorousness.

Every Irish commercial establishment closes at about 1 P.M. on one weekday. This is called early closing day. Visitors heading for a town with an eye to shopping should check on the town's early closing day (in the Irish Tourist Board's *Illustrated Ireland Guide*) or run the risk of finding all the shops there shut up tight.

SOME USEFUL POINTERS

Postal system. Post offices are readily identifiable by their green fronts and the Irish legend *Oifig an Phoist*. They are closed on Sundays. Pillar boxes for the deposit of mail look just like

British ones except that they are painted green instead of red. Postal rates to the United States are as follows: post card by sea, 6 pence; by air, 8 pence; airletter, 9 pence; airmail letter (½ oz.) 15 pence.

Telegraph and Telephone. Telegrams can be filed by telephone or in post offices. Most post offices have telephones, too, and public telephone booths (like the pillar boxes, green in color) are located at strategic points on main streets. Railway and bus stations also have public telephones, as have many pubs, restaurants and goodsized stores. Read the operating instructions carefully, and remember not to push the plunger that drops your money into the box until your party answers. For local calls you will need four pennies; calls between cities always seem, for some reason, to cost 18p. (36 cents), regardless of whether the city called is near or far. There is only one directory for the entire Republic; it is divided into Part 1, covering Dublin and environs, and Part 2, covering the rest of the country. Northern Ireland, too, gets along on one telephone book.

Hours. The Irish are not remarkably early risers: many shops do not open until 9 A.M., and many cafés not until 10 A.M. Banks are open, Monday through Friday, from 10 to 12:30 and again from 1:30 to 3 (5 P.M. on Thursdays). Banks do not open on Saturdays. Pub hours again: in the Republic, weekdays, 10:30 A.M.–11:30 P.M. in summer, and 10:30 A.M.–11 P.M. in winter,

In the heart of Connemara—Ballynahinch Castle, Co. Galway

with time out from 2:30 to 3:30 in Dublin and Cork; Sunday, 12:30–2 P.M. and 4–10 P.M. In Northern Ireland, weekdays 10 A.M.–10 P.M., Sunday closed all day.

Ireland is five hours ahead of Eastern Standard Time and eight hours ahead of Pacific Time.

Newspapers and Magazines. As in Britain, the leading daily newspapers of Ireland are national rather than regional. The *Irish Times* is far and away the best, for its domestic and foreign coverage and literacy. Cheaper, chattier, and more popular are the *Irish Independent* and the *Irish Press,* together with their respective afternoon appendages, the *Evening Herald* and the *Evening Press.* The *Cork Examiner* and the Cork *Evening Echo* are also good national newspapers. There are, in addition, a number of provincial newspapers, mostly weeklies. Most newsstands also carry the leading British dailies *(Express, Daily Mail, Times, Guardian,* etc.). Many Irishmen, oddly, take a British paper—either because its outlook is less insular, or because it costs less! Leading American newspapers are available in Dublin at Eason's, 40 Lower O'Connell Street, and Stanley's, 14 South Leinster Street (branches at several locations). So are the international editions of *Time, Newsweek,* etc. *Hibernia,* published bi-weekly, is an independent and widely read Irish magazine.

Radio and Television. The government-run *Radio-Telefis Eireann* (which means just what you think it does) puts on programs every day, with schedules given in the newspapers. Sampling Irish TV in a pub of an evening, while keeping alert to the natives' reaction thereto, provides interesting insight into Irish attitudes.

Electric current. Electricity in Ireland is AC 220 volts, but many hotels and guesthouses have outlets for electric razors which fit American-style 110-volt plugs. Or you can buy a resistor to adapt your electric razor to Irish current. Available at any large hardware or electrical store, a resistor costs about $5.00.

Tobacco. Tobacco products are taxed heavily in the Republic and even more heavily in Northern Ireland. Irish cigarettes sell for from 25 to 42p. (50¢ to 85¢) for twenty; American brands are hard to find, except in posh hotels, and they are sure to cost even more. The local brands come either plain or tipped, in packs (called packets) of ten or twenty. Both cigars and pipe tobacco cost, on average, about twice as much as in the U. S. or Canada.

Weights and Measures. Although the Irish employ the same terms Americans do for weights and measures there are nevertheless some significant differences as to their meaning. A pint (of Guinness, for instance) is a full fifth larger than the American measure. So is a gallon of gas (petrol). (As for an Irish mile, no one has ever succeeded in defining its precise extent to the satisfaction of all Irishmen!)

Useful Addresses. The United States Embassy occupies a curious circular building at 42 Elgin Road, Ballsbridge, Dublin, tel. 764061. The personnel there are unfailingly kind and courteous, and stand ready to help you out in any legitimate emergency. Other addresses:

Dublin—

AER LINGUS (Irish International Airlines), 41 Upper O'Connell Street. Reservations, tel. 377741; plane information, tel. 370191. Branch offices: 42 Grafton Street and 12 Upper George's Street.

AMERICAN EXPRESS, 116 Grafton Street, tel. 772874.

AUTOMOBILE ASSOCIATION, 23 Suffolk Street, tel. 779481.

BORD FAILTE (Irish Tourist Board), Baggot Street Bridge, tel. 765871.

C.I.E., 59 Upper O'Connell Street.

Train and bus information, tel. 78777; bus tours, tel. 300777.

DUBLIN TOURISM, 51 Dawson Street, tel. 747733.

Cork—

AER LINGUS, 38 Patrick Street, tel. 24331.

AUTOMOBILE ASSOCIATION, 5 South Mall, tel. 20614.

C.I.E., tel. 53411.

Belfast—

AER LINGUS, 46/48 Castle Street, tel. 45151.

AMERICAN EXPRESS, now represented by Hamilton Travel, 23/31 Waring Street, tel. 31321.

AUTOMOBILE ASSOCIATION, Fanum House, Great Victoria Street, tel. 26242.

BOARD FAILTE, 53 Castle Street, tel. 27888.

BRITISH AIRWAYS, Castle Street, tel. 40522.

NORTHERN IRELAND TOURIST BOARD, River House, 48 High Street, tel. 31221.

ULSTERBUS LTD., Minewater Road, tel. 745201.

Train and bus information, tel. 20011.

UNITED STATES CONSULATE, Queen Street, tel. 28239.

CHAPTER 4

DUBLIN AND ENVIRONS

The seaport city of Dublin is on Ireland's east coast and extends north and south of the River Liffey—which empties into Dublin Bay, an arm of the Irish Sea. Its name comes from the Irish *Dubhlinn,* meaning "dark pool", but the site was known even earlier by the city's present official name of Baile Atha Claith ("the town by the hurdle-ford"). First mentioned as a place of importance by Ptolemy (who called it *Eblana)* in 140 A.D., Dublin subsequently became a Viking stronghold, later the center of Norman, and then, English power in Ireland, the site of the 1916 uprising, and finally, the seat of the independent government of Ireland.

With its lovely Georgian squares and spacious greens, its mellow public buildings, churches and monuments, its river and harbor traffic and its busy quays and streets, Dublin is one of the most pleasant of all European capitals. With about half a million inhabitants (closer to a million if its satellite communities are counted in), Dublin is neither too small to offer the amenities appropriate of a proud capital nor so large as to overwhelm the visitor. It is a comfortable city in which a person can easily find his way around. The mountains and the seashore can be reached from the center of the city, by train, bus or car, in no more than twenty minutes.

Getting Oriented

Bisected by the eastward-flowing Liffey, Dublin is also ringed by water; on the north, and almost completely on the south, in the form of canals. On a map, or from the air, the city looks like a landlocked peninsula. The canals, the parallel Ring Roads (North and South) and the North Circular Road, set the practical limits of Dublin. The river and adjacent streets change their names every hundred feet or so. These "quays" or "walks" make up the city's main east-west artery.

Dublin's principal north-south artery is O'Connell Street, a wide thoroughfare lined with 19th century office buildings, stores, and moviehouses. From a lofty statue of Parnell it descends about half a mile, past the General Post Office (G.P.O.) and the site of the now-demolished Nelson's Pillar to an outsize monument to Daniel O'Connell, the Liberator. The wide O'Connell Bridge carries traffic south across the river. There, O'Connell Street becomes Westmoreland Street, which leads, after one block, to College Green; not a green at all, but a wide intersection, with the statue-fronted entrance to famous Trinity College on its eastern flank. From College Green, Dublin's narrow and chic shopping street, Grafton Street, gradually ascends to St. Stephen's Green—a real green, with 22 acres of grass, trees, ponds, fountains and statues, punctuated by flowerbeds. The mile-long stretch between the Parnell statue and St. Stephen's Green, plus the little streets leading off O'Connell and Grafton Streets, make up the city center.

Dromoland Castle, Co. Clare, now one of the world's top hotels

The past in the present—Ennis Abbey, Co. Clare

Getting Around

Without question, the best way to explore central Dublin is on foot. You will have the leisure to observe numerous significant details—of dress or architecture, or behavior—all of which make up the Dublin scene. You hear more: the clop of horses' hoofs, the cawing of gulls, the cries of barrowmen and papersellers, and the soft accent of English as spoken by Dubliners. You even smell more: the fragrance of cut flowers in the flower-stalls, the odor of coal smoke, or the rich aroma of Guinness wafted from the open door of a pub. Another advantage of being on foot is that you are free to follow your nose (or eyes, or ears) as fancy dictates.

However, you may be short of time and want to "do" as much of Dublin as possible. If so, your best bet is to take one (or more) of the C.I.E. sightseeing tours. The best for seeing the city is a three-hour affair that starts at 10 in the morning and again at 3, every day of the week; it costs £1.80 ($3.60) per person. An evening tour, which starts at 6:45 P.M. daily, includes a 1½-hour tour of the capital followed by 2½ hours of "cabaret" at Jury's Hotel in Ballsbridge; the price is £2.20 ($4.40). For roughly one dollar more you can take a twelve-hour tour—there is one to West Wicklow and Kilkenny, and others that include the Slieve Bloom Mountains, or Kennedy Memorial Park.

For only £8.50 per person, you can take a radio train to Killarney which includes train ticket, lunch, high tea, commentary on the sights, and a tour of the Lakes of Killarney in a jaunting car. There is a similar day-trip to Connemara costing about £7.50. Both trips last roughly twelve hours. Only certain dates, May through September. Other tours run out from Busaras (where all tours start) to beauty spots and places of interest outside Dublin—notably Powerscourt, Glendalough, Avoca and the Liffey Valley.

City bus service in Dublin is frequent, fast and inexpensive. The buses operate from 7 A.M. to about midnight. Most begin at O'Connell Bridge and are marked with the names of one of the four quays flanking the bridge—Aston Quay, Bachelor's Walk, Burgh Quay and Eden Quay. Other buses start from O'Connell Street or just off it. The C.I.E. dispatchers stationed at each start- ing point can direct you to the bus you want.

Dublin's taxis do not cruise, but there are cab ranks in the center of O'Connell Street, next to the Bank of Ireland on College Green and on St. Stephen's Green, at the top of Grafton Street. From anywhere else, you can summon a cab by dialing 743333, 766666 or 761111.

Seeing the Town

Before setting out to see Dublin, stop by the Tourist Office and ask for the brochure, *Dublin City* (5 p.). It lists all Dublin's important churches and cathedrals, fine buildings, museums and other cultural and architectural attractions, plus easy walking instructions.

The following is a selection of Dublin landmarks.

Noteworthy Buildings

Dublin Castle stands on high ground off Dame Street, which runs west from Grafton Street. Built by the Normans, between 1208 and 1220, it remained for centuries the principal seat of Norman and English government. The largest remnant of the original structure is the massive tower at the southeast corner; now called the Record Tower, it houses the State Paper Office, a repository of historical documents. The upper castle yard covers the area enclosed by the original walls; in it are the Genealogical Office and the Heraldic Museum. The State Apartments on the south side were once the residence of the English viceroys; the most impressive of them, St. Patrick's Hall, is where Ireland's Presidents are inaugurated. There have been five of them since that office was first established in 1938.

The Custom House, rising from the north bank of the Liffey, near Butt Bridge and just a stone's throw from Busaras, behind it, is considered the finest public building in Dublin. Designed by the celebrated architect James Gandon, it was completed in 1791. Its superbly graceful dome is a central feature of the Dublin skyline.

The Four Courts, further up the Liffey about a mile above O'Connell Bridge, was also designed by Gandon, who took over its construction on the first architect's death. Like the Custom House, it was almost destroyed in the fighting that followed the signing of the Anglo-Irish Treaty of 1921. Again like the Custom House, it has been expertly restored. It now houses the Irish Law Courts.

Notwithstanding its grimy facade, the *Bank of Ireland,* on the north side of College Green, is a pleasing example of stately 18th century architecture. Until the Act of Union of 1800, this low, circular building housed the Irish Parliament. It was begun in 1729. The eastern portico, designed by Gandon, was put up in 1785; the western portico was added between 1792 and 1794.

Trinity College (as mentioned, on the east side of College Green), was founded in 1591 on the site of a priory, which had been suppressed by Henry VIII of England. Founded to further the Reformation in Ireland, the college remained for centuries an exclusively Protestant institution. Among its famous graduates were Edmund Burke, Wolfe Tone, Robert Emmet, Thomas Moore, Isaac Butt and Douglas Hyde. Nowadays, many Trinity undergraduates are Catholics.

Entering the college between statues of Burke and the poet Oliver Goldsmith, you pass under a wide, shady archway where course-meetings and upcoming activities are displayed. Then you emerge into a spacious court, paved with cobblestones and flanked by 18th and 19th century college buildings.

The oldest portion of the college dates from 1722, and the great facade from 1759. The Library, completed in 1732, has a particularly impressive interior. It has on display a number of notable portraits and manuscripts—including the exquisitely illuminated 9th-century devotional Book of Kells, which many consider the most beautiful book ever.

Leinster House, on Kildare Street, just north of St. Stephen's Green, is the present meeting-place of Ireland's parliament, made up of the *Dail* (pronounced "Doyle"), or Chamber of Deputies, and the *Seanad* (Senate). It can be visited, when the Dail is not in session, from 10:30 A.M. to 12:30 P.M. and from 2:30 P.M. to 4:30 P.M. Monday through Friday.

The *General Post Office*—or colloquially the G.P.O.—is the foremost shrine of national independence in the Republic. Originally completed in 1818, it served, nearly a century later, as the headquarters of the Irish Volunteers during the brief Easter

The home of the tall tale—Blarney Castle, Co. Cork

Rebellion of 1916, and was the place where the Republic was proclaimed. During the fighting, the building was shelled by a British gunboat in the Liffey; it was almost completely gutted by fire, but was subsequently rebuilt and restored. Inside, a bronze statue of the dying Cuchulainn commemorates the Irish patriots who died here during the rebellion.

A few other important Dublin buildings should be noted. The Mansion House, a fine Queen Anne-style edifice on Dawson Street, has been the residence of Dublin's Lord Mayors since 1715. The *Catholic Pro-Cathedral,* on Marlborough Street just off O'Connell Street, is an imposing early-19th-century structure in Grecian-Doric style. In the western suburb of Kilmainham stands the *Royal Hospital,* built by a 17th century Duke of Ormonde as a home for old veterans. Across from the hospital's western entrance is *Kilmainham Jail,* in which Irish patriots were imprisoned and the leaders of the 1916 uprising executed. The jail has been converted into a historical museum.

Churches and Cathedrals

Christ Church Cathedral stands south of the Liffey on Lord Edward Street, not far from the Capel Street Bridge. The original structure was begun in 1038 by King Sitric, and Donatus, bishop of Dublin. It was replaced by a great cathedral, founded in 1172, by Strongbow the first Norman conqueror of Ireland. It took half a century to complete. Most of the present structure dates from a restoration carried out between 1871 and 1878, paid for by a wealthy Dublin distiller, Henry Roe.

The cathedral has witnessed a number of historic scenes: 1394, England's Richard II knighted four Irish chieftains—1487, the imposter Lambert Simnel was crowned King Edward VI—1690, James II attended mass on his way to the Battle of the Boyne— and the Protestant King William gave thanks there for his victory in that decisive affray.

Though the cathedral has little exterior ornamentation, inside it is packed with fascinating architectural detail. The 12th century crypt contains statues of Charles II and James II and many historical relics. The cathedral can be visited Monday through Saturday from 9:30 A.M. until 5:30 P.M. in summer, and until 4 P.M. from October through April.

St. Patrick's Cathedral is just a short walk from Christ Church on Patrick Street. It is almost equally venerable having been founded in 1190, though its square tower is of 14th century construction and its spire an 18th century addition. The longest (300 feet) church in Ireland, it contains a great many historical relics.

St. Patrick's is closely associated with Jonathan Swift, the satirist, who was its dean from 1713 to 1745. He and his beloved "Stella" lie buried under the south aisle. Over the robing room door runs his epitaph: "He lies where furious indignation can no longer rend his heart." The cathedral is open to visitors from 9:30 A.M. to 6 P.M. on weekdays, and from 10 A.M. to 4 P.M. on weekends.

St. Michan's Church, on Church Street (north of the Liffey near the Four Courts) was erected in the 17th century on the site of a Danish church, founded in 1096. It contains some exceedingly fine woodwork and a curious 18th century "repentance chair". Its strangest feature is its vaults. Human bodies have lain there for centuries without decomposing—presumably because of the extraordinarily dry atmosphere. The church can be visited from 10 A.M. to 12:45 P.M. and from 2 P.M. to 4:45 P.M. on weekdays, or from 10 A.M. to 12:45 P.M. on Saturdays. Admission to the vaults is 15p. for adults, and 10p. for children under 12.

Also worth a visit are *St. Werburgh's Church,* off Christ

Church Place, and the partially ruined *St. Audóen's Church,* on High Street, close by; both founded by the Normans in the 12th century.

Museums and Galleries

Ireland's *National Museum,* hard by Leinster House, on Kildare Street, is made up of three divisions: Irish Antiquities, Art and Industrial, and Natural History. The first of these is especially noteworthy. Its exhibits vividly recreate Ireland's past, from the Stone Age through medieval times. The display includes a host of interesting artifacts, among them: Bronze Age gold ornaments, the "Tara" Brooch, the heavy silver Ardagh Chalice (both 8th century), and the 12th century Cross of Cong. The Art and Industrial Division includes exhibitions of relics from the 1916–1921 period of intermittent warfare with Britain. The Zoological Section of the Natural History Division (entrance on Merrion Street) contains a fine collection of Irish animals and birds. Museum hours are from 10 A.M. to 5 P.M. weekdays and from 2 P.M. to 5 P.M. Sundays.

The *National Gallery,* around the corner from the National Museum on the western side of Merrion Square, houses a goodly collection of Old Masters. Included are works by Michelangelo, Titian, Tintoretto, Rubens, Van Dyck, Poussin, El Greco and Goya. All the masters of the 17th century Dutch school, except Vermeer, are represented, while the English collection includes no less than ten major works by Gainsborough. In the Irish rooms hang paintings by, among others, John Butler Yeats, father

Galway's splendid new Roman Catholic cathedral

Tranquil Wexford, in the southeast

of the poet and a fine portrait-painter. The *National Portrait Gallery,* housed in the same building, contains portraits of most of Ireland's leading figures over the last three centuries. The building and its collections are open from 10 A.M. to 5 P.M. weekdays, from 10 A.M. to 1 P.M. on Saturdays, and from 2 P.M. to 5 P.M. on Sundays.

The *Municipal Gallery* occupies a particularly handsome Georgian house on the north side of Parnell Square, at the top of O'Connell Street. It contains portraits of the poet Yeats plus a number of his contemporaries who, like him, participated in the Irish Renaissance movement: J. M. Synge, Lady Gregory, Sir Roger Casement, Arthur Griffith, O'Higgins, Hazel Lavery. Other exhibits include a representative collection of paintings by Corot, some Rodin sculptures, and a number of paintings and sculptures by 20th century Irishmen. Hours are 10 A.M.–6 P.M. weekdays, except Monday, until 9 P.M. on Tuesday, and Sundays from September through May, from 11 A.M. to 2 P.M.

The *Civic Museum,* on South William Street, contains historical exhibits relating to Dublin.

One gallery that should not be missed is the magnificent *Trinity College Library,* described briefly before.

Open-Air Markets

For a change of pace and to sample a significant aspect of the local scene, visit at least one of Dublin's several marketplaces. The easiest to reach is in *Moore Street,* just a block west of the G.P.O. Here are fruit, flower and vegetable stalls presided over by big-bosomed ladies who cry their wares—and decry one another's—all at the top of their lungs.

Putting Thirst Things First

Guinness, the rich, dark stout consumed all over Ireland and much of the English-speaking world, has been brewed in Dublin for more than two centuries—on the same spot. The Guinness brewery, on the south bank of the Liffey at the city's western edge, covers 65 acres, employs 3,900 people, and produces three million glassfuls of Guinness a day. It is the biggest brewery in Europe, and is said to export more of its product than any other in the world.

The company offers visits to the brewery from 10 A.M. to 3 P.M. Monday through Friday. A 25 minute film on brewing is shown, and this is followed by a tasting session. Unfortunately, complete tours of the brewery are no longer given. To get to the plant take a No. 78 bus from O'Connell Bridge, or a No. 21 bus from College Green.

A Seedbed of Creativity

Surely no city of comparable size has spawned and nurtured so many first-rate creative talents as has Dublin. The homes and haunts of many illustrious figures are still standing:

Jonathan Swift's birthplace (now gone) stood at 7 Hoey's Court, near St. Patrick's Cathedral where, as mentioned, he was Dean for almost a third of a century. Thomas Moore was born at 12 Aungier Street. Richard Brainsley Sheridan was born in a house (now gone) at 12 Dorset Street. Oscar Wilde was born in 1856 at 21 Westland Row, while George Bernard Shaw was born in the same year at 33 Synge Street. W. B. Yeats was born at 5 Sandymount Avenue, and lived at 42 Fitzwilliam Square from 1928 to 1932. James Joyce was born at 41 Brighton Square West, in the outlying district of Rathgar; he later studied under the Jesuits at University College, Dublin, in the house at 86 St. Stephen's Green. In 1904 he and his friend (and later bitter enemy) Oliver St. John Gogarty shared a martello tower at Sandycove, eight miles from Dublin—now a Joyce museum (see below). Lastly, Brendan Behan was born in 1923 at 14 Russell Street (recently demolished) and grew up to spend time at

The peaceful ruins of Dunbrody Abbey, County Wexford.

several other Dublin addresses, including the Brazen Head (Winetavern Street), Mulligan's (Poolbeg Street), McDaid's (Harry Street), the Bailey (Duke Street), the White Horse (George's Quay) and Mountjoy Prison (North Circular Road).

Behan's best-known play, *The Hostage,* was set in a bawdy-house (now defunct) at 26 Nelson Street. Like many an Irish writer before him, Behan was ignored or vilified by his country-men for years, and had to make a name for himself abroad; in time, however, his mordant comedies came to be staged in his native city.

Dublin's most famous playhouse is the *Abbey Theatre.* The old theatre, on Lower Abbey Street just off O'Connell Street, burned down in 1951. In 1966 it was finally replaced by a splendid new theatre—designed by Ireland's foremost architect, Michael Scott. He also designed *Busaras,* the Cork Opera House, and several other handsome public buildings that have gone up in Ireland in the last decade. The Abbey's rivals in Dublin are the *Gaiety,* on South King Street, the *Gate,* on Parnell Square, the *Olympia,* in Dame Street, and the *Eblana,* in the basement of Busaras. In addition to excellent productions, a particular delight of theatre-going in Dublin is the low cost: tickets range from 50 pence to £2 and can be obtained at the box office from 10:30 A.M. to 6 P.M. Plays are presented nightly, except Sundays, throughout the year.

"The boys" have a "jar" at Mulligan's, Dublin

Majestic Westport House, Co. Mayo

Other Organized Entertainment

Aside from plays and movies, Dublin does not offer a remarkable variety of after-dark entertainment. There are, to be sure, greyhound races six nights a week. Lectures and concerts are constantly put on; for dates, times and places consult a newspaper, or the free booklet *Events of the Week*. Then too, you can take a C.I.E. evening tour—or a cruise on Dublin Bay. But most non-theatrical evening entertainment centers around cabaret (in its special local sense of "Irish Nights") and ballad-singing.

For Irish-style cabaret your best bet is Jury's Cabaret, which starts nightly at 8:30 at Jury's Hotel on College Green. The 2½-hour variety show costs £2. Dinner is served at 7:30, and the all-in price of that plus the cabaret is £6, and the drinks cost no more than elsewhere.

The Legion of Mary also stages Irish Nights two or three evenings a week from early June through September: dates, hours and locations are posted in the O'Connell Street Tourist Office. Though performed entirely by amateurs they are usually very good, and invariably inspired with winning enthusiasm. There is no charge whatever, though a small contribution is quite in order.

As for ballad-singing, the best place for it in all Ireland is the Abbey Tavern in the town of Howth, on a peninsula jutting out into Dublin Bay. The Abbey is so popular with both visitors and natives, that you had better reserve a table—if possible at least a day in advance (telephone 322006). Admission is 50p. The

Abbey Singers' show, from 8:30 P.M. to 11:30 P.M. (Sundays 8–10 P.M.) is a heady mixture of melodious Irish voices and "instrumental" music—on fiddles, spoons, "uileann" pipes and tin whistles.

For those who love Irish folk music— jigs, reels and the rest—there are the music clubs, alternately known as traditional music clubs. The meetings of these groups are well off the standard tourist beat, but they are not closed affairs, and visitors are welcomed to them with great cordiality.

There are a number of regular weekly sessions of various branches of the national music association, Comaltas Ceoltoiri Eireann, in and around Dublin. These groups, who sing traditional Irish music, meet in different places: at the time of writing there is a weekly Sunday session at the North Star Hotel, Amiens Street, a Saturday session at St. Vincent's School, Glasnevin, as well as a Friday evening meeting in Finglas. But changes of day and scene are not uncommon, so be sure to check in advance with Comaltas (tel. 757554). The same organization or the Irish Tourist Board can also tell you about the numerous Ceilis—informal Irish traditional dancing evenings—held in the Dublin area. On Saturday nights the Piper's Club holds sessions from 9 to 1 at 14 Thomas Street. Admission is just 15 pence.

The Ould Triangle Folk Club, at 81 Lower Mount Street, meets on Wednesday, Friday and Sunday nights. Admission is 15 pence (35 cents), and both the folk music and the listeners are less exclusively Irish and more international.

Tailors' Hall is the 18th century hall of the old Tailors' Guild of Dublin. It has been excellently restored by the Irish Georgian Society and is now hosting an evening in which your entrance, a light meal with wine and some song are all included in a £1 charge.

Unorganized Entertainment: The Pubs

Dublin is famous around the world for its rich variety of pub life. That fame is not founded on the elaborateness or elegance of the city's drinking places, many of which are quite small and simple, but rather, on that something called atmosphere—chiefly supplied by the people in front of and behind the bar.

Basic facts about drinking in Ireland, plus tips on pub behavior, have been given before. Below is a list of some of the more central—and, hopefully, interesting pubs of the more than one thousand in the city.

The *Brazen Head*, on Winetavern Street just south of Usher's Quay, is a charming, if somewhat down-at-heel, chunk of Irish history. First licensed to sell liquor in 1666, it very probably is, as it claims to be, the oldest pub in the land. Picturesquely located off a stone-paved courtyard, it consists of a low-ceilinged room lighted by dim brass-bound lanterns. Over the centuries,

Burke, Emmet, Wolfe Tone and O'Connell all allegedly stayed a night or more in the rooms upstairs.

Davy Byrne's, at 21 Duke Street off Grafton Street, a block from College Green, is familiar to Joyceans as the place where Leopold Bloom stopped for a drink on that memorable June 16, 1904. The pub is much grander now, with a softly-lighted cocktail lounge in back, and the clientele is smart and cosmopolitan. Cold Munich beer is a house specialty. Davy Byrne's is a good place to take a break from shopping in Grafton Street.

Bartley Dunne's, at 32 Lower Stephen Street, is a favorite hangout of students. The big room at the rear is richly and comfortably furnished; the atmosphere pleasant and easy.

The Long Hall, 51 South Great George's Street, takes its name from the extraordinarily narrow snug that runs its entire length. The pub's walls are lined with splendid gilt-trimmed mirrors, and heavy crystal chandeliers hang from the ceilings. A centuries-old clock, paintings in massive frames, pewter pitchers, china dishes and assorted bric-a-brac complete the scene. Most of the people you will find there will be workingmen and their wives who live in the neighborhood.

Tranquil Jerpoint Abbey, Co. Kilkenny

McDaid's, on the tiny street called Harry Street that runs west from Grafton Street, is known as "the poet's pub". The decor is nondescript Edwardian, but the atmosphere is cheery, and the talk—overheard or participated in—can be most entertaining.

Mooney's. This name denotes a chain, and Mooney's pubs are to be found at several Dublin locations. They are quite plain, but also quite good. You are likely to run into fewer fellow-tourists in a Mooney's than you might elsewhere.

Neary's, at 1 Chatham Street, whose back door faces the stage door of the Gaiety Theatre, is the haunt of actors, playwrights and drama critics. Its decor is plush Edwardian, and the oysters served therein are delicious.

O'Donoghue's, at 15 Merrion Row, traditionally a center for folk music, is no longer the haven for jeans-clad long-haired young people it once was. The music is still good, but the clientele is getting older.

O'Dwyer's, at 104 Lower Leeson Street, is a gathering place for the students of University College, Dublin (U.C.D.).

The Pearl, at 37 Fleet Street, is patronized by, among others, the staff of *The Irish Times,* whose head office is close by.

The Scotch House, on Burgh Quay, is another favorite with Dublin newspapermen.

Searson's, on Upper Baggot Street, is a tasteful, modern place, not unlike a good American big-city bar.

Toner's, a block from O'Donoghue's on Merrion Row, is much frequented by Dublin's art students and art-oriented people in general.

What to See Around Dublin
There is not too much to attract the visitor immediately west or north of the city, though you might like to mosey around The Good Old Days Museum in Rush, about 12 miles to the north of Dublin. This nostalgic display of 19th and 20th century vehicles and machinery is the brainchild of Liam Butterfly and attracts 50,000 visitors annually. In the same general direction, the drive to Drogheda by way of Malahide, Skerries and Balbriggan offers some fine views of the Irish Sea. But the region south of the capital is another matter: southern County Dublin and (especially) County Wicklow contain mile after mile of magnificent scenery, and abound in places of interest. The following are the most noteworthy places within easy reach of Dublin.

The *James Joyce Museum* is housed in a martello tower that was built early in the 19th century as a fortification against a Napoleonic invasion (that never came). It stands on a cliff overlooking Dublin Bay at Sandycove, eight miles southeast of O'Connell Bridge. For a short time in 1904, Joyce and Oliver St. John Gogarty lived in the tower; the two were later to emerge, in the pages of *Ulysses,* as Stephen Dedalus and Buck Mulligan, respectively.

In the tower's ground floor hang paintings showing scenes from *Ulysses.* On the floor above is a collection of Joyce mem- orabilia—the author's letters and manuscripts, his cane and cig- arette box. From the parapet at the top there is a very fine view of the sea and coast. The museum is open, Monday through Saturday, from 10 A.M. to 1 P.M. and from 2 P.M. to 5 P.M. and on Sunday from 3 P.M. to 6 P.M. Admission is 5p. (12 cents).

The *Powerscourt Demesne and Gardens,* on the edge of the picturesque village of Enniskerry, is a beautiful estate. The majestic 18th-century manor house, formerly the home of the aristocratic Powerscourt family was gutted by fire in 1974, but the lovely Italian and Japanese Gardens together with 34,000 acres of grounds in lovely, rolling country are open to the public. The demesne includes the 400-foot-high Powerscourt Waterfall, the highest in Britain and Ireland. Powerscourt gardens are open daily from 10:30 to 5:30 between Easter and the end of October; admission is 35 pence for adults and 20 pence for children. The waterfall and deerpark are open from 10 to 8 all year round, and admission to these is 15 pence for adults and 10 pence for children.

Glendalough, 32 miles south of Dublin in the Wicklow Mountains, is a beautiful valley celebrated for its historical and archeological interest. Here, in the 6th century, St. Kevin founded a monastery, which grew into the monastic city of Glendalough, one of the most renowned centers of learning in Europe. In the 9th and 10th centuries the city was plundered by the Danes. In the 12th century St. Laurence O'Toole was the abbot of Glendalough; he later became archbishop of Dublin, and is the patron saint of that city. In 1398 most of Glendalough was burned by the English and left in ruins.

With its large and varied clusters of remains around the Upper and Lower Lakes (Glendalough means, in Irish, the Glen of the Two Lakes), this valley is of outstanding interest to all students of the past—professional or amateur. The eerie, mystical aura of the scene makes a visit to Glendalough unforgettable.

Robertstown, 28 miles west of Dublin, is a small village which drew its life from trade on the Grand Canal. The Canal has been closed to commercial traffic for a number of years, but recently the village renewed itself as a tourist center. It has an excellent festival the first two weeks of August, and candlelight banquets every night from May to September. The evening starts at 7:30 P.M. with a visit to the Falconry of Ireland, now world-famous for its collection of hunting birds, and continues with a leisurely horsedrawn barge cruise on the Grand Canal. This is followed by a candlelight banquet in the Grand Canal Hotel and traditional Irish entertainment. The all-in cost of the evening is £4.75.

CHAPTER 5
THE SOUTH

In Ireland, "the North" means the Six Counties, or Northern Ireland, and "the West", the province of Connacht plus County Donegal on the north and (sometimes) County Clare on the south. "The South" is a vaguer term: it can mean either the province of Munster, with or without County Clare, or either of these regions plus the counties of southern Leinster that comprise the southeastern part of the island. ("The East" is a term that is seldom, if ever, used in Ireland.) For the purposes of this chapter, "the South" will be considered that part of Ireland lying south of a line connecting Dublin, with Limerick, and outside the central plain.

The South of Ireland is a remarkably varied region, abounding in natural beauty. The Wicklow Hills, mentioned at the end of the last chapter, rise south of Dublin; further south lies Ireland's "Sunny Southeast", with the ports of Wexford and Waterford looking out, respectively, on St. George's Channel and the Atlantic. West of Waterford rise the Comeragh and Knockmealdown Mountains; north of the latter group rises the majestic Rock of Cashel, perhaps the most sacred spot in all Ireland. Further west along the coast is the Republic's second city, Cork, and, just north of it, Ireland's single greatest tourist attraction, the world-famous Blarney Stone at Blarney Castle.

County Cork is the largest of Ireland's 26 or, if Northern Ireland is included, 32 counties. Its western part and County Kerry together form Ireland's fabled Southwest, a region of quite extraordinary beauty. In the Southwest are mountainous peninsulas thrusting westward into the Atlantic, with lovely, fjord-like bays between them; sudden, unexpected patches of lush, subtropical vegetation; and some of the most beautiful lakes in the world. East of County Kerry, in the north, County Limerick marches along the broad Mouth of the Shannon to historic Limerick, Eire's third largest city.

Ireland's South is justly famous for its seacoast, dotted with picturesque fishing villages, but some of the region's most attractive places lie inland. On the pages that follow the high points of Ireland's South will be briefly described in a roughly east-to-west order—that is, from the standpoint of a traveler setting out to explore the region from Dublin.

County Wexford occupies the southeast corner of Ireland. Its capital is the ancient seaport of **Wexford** (population 11,849), located where the River Slaney broadens into Wexford Harbor. The site of a Viking settlement, Wexford City was seized by the Normans in 1169. In 1649 Cromwell captured the town and butchered its inhabitants. Wexford's finest hour came a century and a half later, during the 1798 uprising, when its citizens expelled the British garrison and held out, against overwhelming odds, for nearly a month.

Wexford is so compact that it has no local buses; the people get around on foot. A good tour starting-point is Crescent Quay, at the midpoint of the town's waterfront. The Irish Tourist Office is there; across from it stands a statue of Commodore John Barry, who is credited with being the founder of the U. S. Navy.

In County Wexford, the late John F. Kennedy and his late brother Robert F. Kennedy were considered "two of their own", for their great-grandfather, Patrick Kennedy, was a Wexford farmer. He emigrated to the U.S. from New Ross, just 23 miles from Wexford City. When the President visited Wexford he laid a wreath at the base of the Barry statue.

Wexford's narrow Main Street runs parallel to the quay. At its northern end is a broad intersection known as the *Bull Ring,* where bloodthirsty Norman noblemen once indulged their favorite pastime of bull-baiting. In the Bull Ring stands a fine statue of an embattled pikeman, symbolizing Wexford's hopeless, gallant stand in 1798.

In and around Wexford are several interesting reminders of bygone days. *Westgate Tower,* the only remaining fortified gateway of the original town wall, stands at the north end. Close by are the ruins of pre-Norman *Selskar (St. Sepulchre's) Abbey;* there, the first Anglo-Irish treaty was signed, in 1169, when Wexford surrendered to Robert Fitzstephen. Three years later, Henry II spent Lent within its walls, doing penance for the murder of Thomas à Becket. Johnstown Castle, 3½ miles south of Wexford, was built in the 13th century, partly destroyed by Cromwell, and rebuilt in the 19th century. It is now an agricultural institute, and its pleasant grounds are open to the public.

The "English Baronies" of Forth and Bargy, extending south from Wexford Harbor to Bannow Bay, were the first part of Ireland to be settled by Anglo-Normans. The district abounds in castles, ruined abbeys and churches.

The *Saltee Islands,* off the south coast of County Wexford, constitute Ireland's foremost bird sanctuary, with a huge population of puffins, razorbills, kittiwakes and other sea birds. The two islands can be reached from the village of Kilmore Quay by a boat, operated by Mr. Eamonn Doyle, when weather and tides permit. Arrangements should be made in advance.

Every year, in October, Wexford plays host to an eight-day Festival of Opera. Operas are staged and opera films shown. In addition, there are sailing races, hurling matches, an Irish music concert and pictorial exhibitions.

Landlocked **County Kilkenny,** a region of undulating plains and low hills, lies west of Wexford and southwest of Dublin. The county has much lovely scenery, especially along the Nore and Barrow Rivers. Its capital is **Kilkenny** (population 9,838). Beautifully situated on the Nore River, Kilkenny is a particularly charming town, with narrow, winding streets and numerous ancient buildings in a fine state of preservation.

The capital of the pre-Norman kingdom of Ossory, Kilkenny was named for St. Canice, who built a church there in the 6th

The River Shannon at Limerick, King John's Castle at right

century. ("Kil"—or, in Irish, *cill*—means a church or cell, and the old name, *Cill Cainnis,* eventually became Kilkenny.) From 1293 to 1408 the town was the meeting-place of many Anglo-Norman parliaments: in 1366, the Statute of Kilkenny was passed, prescribing stiff penalties for any Anglo-Norman who adopted Irish speech, dress or customs, or who married an Irishwoman. After about 1400 the town was the principal seat of the powerful Butler family—Earls, later Dukes, and now Marquesses of Ormonde (Ormonde = East Munster). Kilkenny's most glorious period was from 1642 to 1648, when the Confederation of Kilkenny functioned as an independent Irish parliament.

Kilkenny's two most imposing structures stand at opposite ends of the town: *St. Canice's Cathedral* on high ground at the north, and *Kilkenny Castle* by a bend in the River Nore, at the south. Between these majestic buildings, both 13th century, are a number of smaller historic buildings—along the High Street, or just off it. After calling at the centrally-located Irish Tourist Office at the Parade Kilkenny, you could spend the better part of a day viewing the town's attractions. Starting at the cathedral, make your way gradually south to the castle with a stop en route for a bite, possibly at Kyteler's Inn, the oldest house in Kilkenny.

St. Canice's Cathedral contains a great many fine medieval monuments, including the tombs of several Earls of Ormonde. The earliest dated monument bears the date 1285. Next to the cathedral stands the 100-foot Round Tower, a relic of an even more ancient church, possibly the one St. Canice founded.

The Dominican Church, on Blackmill Street, incorporates the tower and 14th-century windows of the Black Abbey (Dominican)—built there in 1225 by William le Mareschal, Earl of Pembroke. To the east stands the Black Freren Gate, the only remaining gate of the medieval town walls. Further along Abbey Street, and across Parliament Street, are the ruins of the *Grey Friary* (Franciscan) founded in 1234.

Recently-restored Rothe House, now a museum, is on Parliament Street. Nearby is the handsome 18th-century Tholsel, or Town Hall, on High Street, and *Kyteler's Inn,* on St. Kieran's Street. This last building was the home of Dame Alice Kyteler, a wealthy lady who, after surviving four husbands, was accused in 1324 of witchcraft. She escaped, but her maid Petronilla, was convicted and burned to death in her stead. The house was in use as an inn as early as 1639, and is, today, Kilkenny's foremost hostelry.

Kilkenny Castle remained in the possession of successive heads of the Butler family until 1966, when the Marquess of Ormonde presented it to the Kilkenny Corporation. The voluminous Ormonde Manuscripts—a treasure-trove of historical lore—have been transferred to the National Library in Dublin. As mentioned in the "Shopping" section of Chapter 3 the castle's former stables and grooms' quarters have in recent years been converted into workshops. Artisans of the National Design Centre utilize ancient Irish designs to create a variety of useful and ornamental things. For anyone interested in fine design, a visit to the well-laid-out showrooms amply justifies a trip to Kilkenny.

Beer has been brewed at Kilkenny longer than in any other place in Ireland. Every year, in the merry month of May, the town puts on an annual Kilkenny Beer Festival, featuring any amount of fiddling, dancing, singing and—you guessed it—beer-drinking.

County Waterford, west of County Wexford on Ireland's south coast, combines scenic beauty of many kinds. Its shoreline is a series of rugged headlands and sand-fringed bays. Much of its interior is mountainous. It is bounded on the west by the *Black-water Valley,* containing Ireland's finest river scenery, and on the north by the pleasant River Suir.

After receiving the waters of the Nore and the Barrow, the Suir opens out into Waterford Harbor. There, on the south bank, stands the fine old city of **Waterford** (population 31,968), the fourth largest in the Irish Republic. Its name is derived from *Vadrefjord,* the name bestowed on it by the Vikings who established a settlement there in the year 853.

In time, the Danish occupiers were Christianized, and about 1030 their leader, Reginald, is said to have built Waterford's first church. In 1170 the Anglo-Norman conqueror Strongbow took the town by storm. Thereafter, Waterford remained for several centuries second only to Dublin in importance among the Anglo-Norman strongholds in Ireland.

The most conspicuous and interesting building in Waterford is *Reginald's Tower,* a round structure with a four-foot-thick wall that stands at the downstream end of The Quay, at the foot of the wide thoroughfare called The Mall. Erected in 1003 as part of the Danes' city defenses, it was later used as a prison for political offenders, and, under King John of Magna Carta fame, as a mint. In the 19th century it became a prison again.

Today, Reginald's Tower contains an interesting historical exhibit which includes the original charters granted to the city by medieval kings and queens of England. Mrs. June Gloster will be pleased to show you around. Nearby, at 41 The Quay, is the Waterford Tourist Office where you can arrange for a visit to the famous Waterford Glass Factory on the edge of town.

Reputed burial place of St. Patrick Downpatrick, Co. Down

Around the world, the name of Waterford is associated with fine handcut glass- and crystal-ware. The much-prized Waterford glass was first produced between 1783 and 1851. In 1952, after a lapse of more than a century, production was resumed, utilizing the famous old patterns of Georgian days. This revival has been so successful that deliveries are now a year behind orders.

For 16 days every September Waterford puts on a unique festival, the Festival of Light Opera. Amateur light opera groups come from England, Scotland, Wales and the Irish hinterlands to compete for the Waterford Glass Trophy. They can all be seen—from good seats—for the low cost of £20, the price of a season ticket.

County Tipperary—best known, perhaps, for the famous ballad sung by British Tommies in World War I—extends north from the River Suir to Lough Derg, a long, wide stretch of the River Shannon. Ireland's largest inland county, Tipperary contains varied scenery (mountains, hills, plains, river valleys) and several interesting antiquities, notably the celebrated Rock of Cashel.

The county's chief town, **Clonmel** (population 11,622) stands on the north bank of the Suir, just across from County Waterford. Clonmel is a place of indefinable but very real charm. Long a stronghold of the Earls of Ormonde, the town is notable for having put up the stiffest resistance of Cromwell that that invader encountered anywhere in Ireland. It is also remembered as the birthplace of that engaging writer, Laurence Sterne, author of *Tristram Shandy*.

Fifteen miles northwest of Clonmel is the small town of *Cashel* (population 2,679). While there are many other points of interest in and around Cashel, which you can learn about by stopping off at the tourist office in the Town Hall, most visitors come to view the remarkable ecclesiastical remains crowning the *Rock of Cashel*, a limestone outcrop that rises 200 feet above the plain north of the town.

Cashel was the seat of Munster kings from about 370 until 1101, when King Murtagh O'Brien granted the Rock to the Church. In 450, St. Patrick baptised King Aengus and his brothers there. In 977 the great Brian Boru was crowned king of Munster at Cashel. On its being granted to the Church, the Rock was dedicated to "God, St. Patrick and St. Ailbhe".

Buildings on the Rock include a 10th-century round tower, Cormac's Chapel (built by a memorable 12th-century king-bishop of Cashel), the Cathedral, the Hall of Vicars Choral and St. Patrick's Cross.

County Cork, Ireland's largest county, extends west from the picturesque old port and seaside resort of *Youghal* (pronounced "yawl"), of which Sir Walter Raleigh was once mayor, to the tips of the westward-thrusting peninsulas enclosing *Bantry Bay*. On the north, undulating limestone lands, interrupted by river valleys, extend to the borders of Kerry, Limerick and Tipperary.

The county's main center is, of course, **Cork,** the Republic's second largest city (population 128,645). Straddling the River Lee, which divides and reunites in such a way that it requires 14 bridges, Cork spreads outward to climb the slopes of the surrounding hills. These heights offer panoramic views of the city.

Cork's history goes back to the 6th century, when St. Finbarr founded a church and school on the Lee. In 820 Norse invaders burned St. Finbarr's city but returned a few years later to establish a settlement there. Three and a half centuries later Cork became an Anglo-Norman stronghold. In 1690 Sir Winston Churchill's great ancestor, the first Duke of Marlborough, besieged Cork and forced the garrison to surrender to King William III (William of Orange).

Cork has a long history of resistance to invaders and occupiers, earning the sobriquet of "rebel Cork". In the mid-19th century, it was a principal center of the Fenian movement. It also figured prominently in the 1919–21 War of Independence. Corkmen are celebrated in Ireland for their stubbornness and canniness; perhaps significantly, the present Prime Minister of Eire, Jack Lynch, is a Corkman.

Glengarriff Bay, County Cork.

The city's main thoroughfare is crescent-shaped St. Patrick Street, alternately known as Patrick Street, which runs from St. Patrick's Bridge to a broad paved expanse called the Grand Parade. A short walk from St. Patrick Street is Cork's most famous landmark, the church of St. Anne's, Shandon, with its

> . . . *Bells of Shandon*
> *That sound so grand on*
> *The pleasant waters of the River Lee.*

The Irish Tourist Office, situated at Monument Buildings, Grand Parade, will gladly supply information on local points of interest and help visitors to secure accommodations. That eminently useful Irish Tourist Office publication, the *Illustrated Ireland Guide*, gives details of four recommended walks within the city.

C.I.E. tours out of Cork enable visitors to view the greater part of Ireland's Southwest—including the fabled Ring of Kerry and Bantry Bay—in the space of a single day. For times and prices (top price: £3 or $6), consult the C.I.E. "Day Trips" leaflet, available at the Tourist Board office and the C.I.E. bus station.

Thanks to the Irish love of theatre in all its forms, Cork, despite its relatively small size, is a considerable cultural center. The Southern Theatre Group stages the works of contemporary Irish playwrights. During the summer its productions can be seen nightly either at the magnificent new Opera House, or at Father Matthew Hall (named for a martyr, Father Matthew Sheehy, who was tried and executed in Cork in 1766). There is no dearth of local talent for Irish Nights, either. Among the special annual events in Cork is the International Choral Festival, held in May—a week of choral singing, alternating with folk-dancing. In June there's the Cork Summer Show and Industrial Exhibition—a combined cattle fair, horse, dog and flower shows lasting three days. Undoubtedly the main event is the Cork Film International, held in June. It is not as glamorous as the festivals at Cannes or Venice, but every bit as worthwhile—it is also very much less expensive: £5 ($10.00) admits a visitor to eight days of screening, plus eight parties. Although feature films are shown, the competition for the coveted St. Finbarr statuettes and the Waterford Glass Trophy is among short films only.

Just five miles north of Cork, by a clearly-marked road, is the village of **Blarney,** with *Blarney Castle* and its celebrated *Blarney Stone.* According to legend it instantly bestows the gift of witty, brilliant conversation upon anyone who kisses it. For reasons that become clear on the site, the kissing has to be done upside-down. It's worth doing, if only to be able to say you've done it; and to take care of doubters in advance, you can have your picture taken in the act.

Another worthwhile side-trip from Cork takes you south 18 miles to the picturesque fishing village of **Kinsale** (population 1,622). Kinsale received its first charter from Edward III, in 1333. In 1601 a Spanish force sailed into the harbor, took the town, and held it against English forces under Mountjoy. The Irish Earls of Tyrone and Tirconnell marched from the north to help, but in the end the Spaniards surrendered. These historic events are commemorated by a particularly noteworthy pub, *The Spaniard*—a "must" stop for all visitors to Kinsale.

Among the many notable antiquities of Kinsale is *St. Multose Church,* built in the 12th century and still in use; inside it, the old town stocks can be seen. There are also the remains of a Carmelite Friary built in 1314. Fifteenth century *Desmond Castle* is worth exploring, as is the town museum in the "new" Courthouse.

In West Cork there are interesting towns, villages and beauty spots, but unless you have plenty of time you will probably want to push on to Ireland's fabled Southwest. From Cork, head for Glengarriff, on Bantry Bay, either by way of Macroom (62 miles) or by the even more scenic route that leads through Bandon, Dunmanway and Bantry (68 miles).

Glengarriff (population 244) occupies a spectacularly beautiful setting in a deep, secluded valley at the head of Bantry Bay. The narrow valley is thickly wooded, with luxuriant Mediterranean flora in the more sheltered places. Glengarriff Harbor is guarded at the entrance by *Garinish Island,* a mile offshore. Garinish is justly famous for its exquisite gardens, and the short and inexpensive (25p. or 50 cents) trip there is well worth the time and effort.

From Glengarriff, Route L61 follows the shoreline north; then, from little Adrigole, Route L62 climbs the *Slieve Mishkish Mountains* to the *Healy Pass.* Ahead lies Kenmare, Killarney and all of County Kerry.

County Kerry occupies the southwestern corner of Ireland. Except in the north, where it slopes gently down to the mouth of the Shannon, it is made up of rugged uplands. It is, in fact, the most mountainous of Irish counties: *Carrantuohill* (3,414 feet), in the range called Macgillycuddy's Reeks, is Ireland's highest mountain. The county's Atlantic coastline is deeply indented by bays. Inland, the intramontane valleys contain streams, rivers and lakes, including the breathtakingly beautiful *Lakes of Killarney.*

Because **Killarney** (population, 7,184) is located on these lakes at about equal distance from Kerry's three westward-pointing fingers of land (south to north, the Beara, Iveragh and Dingle Peninsulas), it is the natural center for a tour of Ireland's Southwest. Killarney is poetically nicknamed "Heaven's Reflex". The Irish Tourist Office is on Main Street, in the Town Hall; ask for the "Killarney" folder, which lists several established tours of the district. These tours, all with guides, are conducted, variously, in buses, cars and colorful, horse-drawn "jaunting cars".

If this makes Killarney sound rather "touristy," it can't be helped; catering to thousands of visitors every summer, the town inevitably displays certain tourist characteristics, including a plethora of souvenir shops. This should not put anyone off— the nearby lakes and surrounding country, which inspired Wordsworth, Thackeray and Tennyson to flights of poetic ecstasy, remain, today, as lovely and unmarred as ever.

There is so much to see in County Kerry that it is hard to know which road to take from Killarney. But a person without much time could do no better than to tour the so-called *Ring of*

Kerry, either on his own or with a group. The "Ring" is an excellent road that runs all around the broad and majestic **Iveragh Peninsula.** Starting and ending at Killarney, the tour covers 110 miles; it lasts, with stops, including a long one for lunch, the better part of a day. You will see an astonishing variety of scenery—towering mountains; magnificent seascapes, with sand-fringed coves and off-shore islands; rugged headlands and capes; broad peat bogs, with neatly-stacked piles of cut turf; villages, towns, and lonely whitewashed cottages, the abandoned ones standing open to the sky; clumps of lush subtropical foliage, flourishing under the benign influence of the Gulf Stream; and lastly the three incomparable Lakes of Killarney.

The most interesting historical remains in the Killarney district are probably those of *Ross Castle* on the Lower Lake. This well-preserved ruin, dating from the 14th century, is one of the finest examples of castle-building in Kerry.

Killorglin (population 1,100), 14 miles west of Killarney, is the site of a unique fair, the "Puck Fair and Pattern", usually held from the 10th to the 12th of August. On the first day of the fair a large billy goat, his horns bedecked with ribbons and rosettes, is borne in triumph, in a commodious cage, to a raised platform in the center of the town square. There he is enthroned, as King Puck, to preside over the great cattle, sheep and horse fair and the attendant merrymaking.

If time permits, a visit to the most northerly of Kerry's promontories, the **Dingle Peninsula,** is definitely recommended. The scenery is wondrously wild and rugged. Many of the inhabitants of the peninsula's western part still speak Gaelic, and some (at Ballydavid) still build wood-and-canvas curraghs according to a pattern many centuries old. Off the tip of the peninsula can be seen the westernmost bits of Europe, the *Blasket Islands;* now uninhabited, they used to be known as "the nearest parish to America".

Tralee (population 12,289) at the foot of the peninsula, is the chief town of Kerry, and the inspiration of the world-famous song, *The Rose of Tralee.* From there, Route T68 heads north to the shore of the Shannon estuary, where it bends east and heads for Limerick.

The seaport of **Limerick** (population 57,161), Eire's third largest city, stands by the Shannon at the point where that great river becomes tidal. Only 15 miles from Shannon Airport (in County Clare), Limerick is often the first Irish city that many transatlantic visitors see.

Limerick is an old city. In the 9th century, Danish invaders established a settlement on the site as a base for inland raids. They were finally driven out by Brian Boru, but the Irish were again ousted by the Anglo-Normans. In 1210 King John visited Limerick and ordered a strong fortress built there—part of which is still standing. Twice during the 17th century pro-Stuart garrisons at Limerick had to surrender—in 1651 to Cromwell's General Ireton, and in 1691, to General Ginkel of King William's army. A year before the latter affray the defenders, under Patrick Sarsfield, had successfully held off a huge force under King William himself; when Limerick at last surrendered, William was generous. In the Treaty of Limerick he allowed the garrison to march out with full honors, and guaranteed religious freedom to Catholics. Subsequently, however, the English Parliament repudiated the treaty, and in the ensuing decades the Catholic Irish were so sorely oppressed that nearly half a million Irishmen left their homeland to fight for the Catholic kings of France and Spain. Thus Limerick came to be known by the melancholy title of "the City of the Violated Treaty".

Modern Limerick was first laid out in the orderly 18th century so that, unlike most Irish aggregations, it is made up of regular blocks; streets and cross-streets intersect at regular intervals, at right angles. The city's central artery, about three-quarters of a mile long, is broad O'Connell Street. The Irish Tourist Office is at 62 O'Connell Street.

Limerick's single most interesting building is *King John's Castle,* at the north end of the city, overlooking the Shannon. Although it has undergone many alterations since the 13th century and was severely battered by General Ginkel's artillery, the greater part of it remains intact. Across the Thomond Bridge from it, in County Clare, stands the *Treaty Stone,* an irregular block of limestone on which the "violated" treaty is said to have been signed.

A particularly curious old structure is *St. Mary's Cathedral* (Church of Ireland). It was founded about 1194, when Donal Mor O'Brien donated his own castle for the purpose. Presumably, parts of the castle were incorporated in the building, which differs in several details from other churches of the period. Inside are a number of interesting old objects. Part of the boundary wall of the cathedral grounds was once the front of the 17th century Exchange. In that building stood a pedestal on which city merchants paid their debts—a custom which gave rise to the expression "paying on the nail". The original "nail" is now in the *Limerick Museum* in the Carnegie Library, just outside the People's Park at the other end of the city.

Although there is much to see in the rural parts of County Limerick, most visitors, when they have seen the city, head south to Killarney, east to Dublin, or west, across the Shannon, to County Clare—and on into Ireland's wild, beautiful West.

CHAPTER 6

For the purposes of this chapter, the West of Ireland will be considered as the entire region between the River Shannon and the Atlantic, together with County Donegal, at the island's northwest corner.

This area is so varied topographically it is difficult to describe it in general terms. When contrasted to the rest of Ireland, however, certain distinctive characteristics emerge. The West is less developed industrially, less intensively cultivated and less densely populated than the country as a whole. Being far removed from the centers of Anglo-Norman and English power, it remained less affected culturally by centuries of foreign occupation. Along its western fringe—the Gaeltacht, or Gaelic-speaking area—the old Irish language is still heard and old Irish folkways survive. Inevitably, Synge, Yeats and the other literary apostles of the Irish Renaissance sought inspiration there. Altogether, Ireland's hauntingly beautiful West is the most primitive, the most romantic, and the most *Irish* region in the land.

At the same time, the West is the region of Ireland where the Spanish influence is most predominant—in family names, such as Costello, and in the faces of the people. Galway, in particular, was the Irish terminus of a brisk trade between Hibernia and Iberia that began in the Middle Ages. And many sailors from the ships of the Spanish Armada, wrecked off Ireland in 1588, survived to intermarry with the women of Ireland's West.

As his plane descends at Shannon, an American visitor gets his first glimpse of Ireland close up: it is southernmost **County Clare,** by the River Shannon's broad mouth. From the airport, the road to Limerick first passes an ultramodern industrial complex (sponsored by the quasi-governmental Shannon Development Board) and then 15th century Bunratty Castle, now restored to its original appearance. The experience serves as a fitting introduction to Clare, a county of some startling contrasts.

Bounded on the east by Lough Derg and the Shannon, on the south by the Shannon estuary, on the west by the Atlantic and on the north by Galway Bay, Clare is almost an island. It's capital and chief town, **Ennis** (population 5,972) lies athwart the road from Limerick to Galway. Clare is famous for its splendid seacoast, with the towering Cliffs of Moher; for its eerie, desert-like Burren district; also for the two places mentioned before— Shannon Airport and Bunratty Castle.

Bunratty Castle, about ten miles from Limerick and five from Shannon Airport, is the scene of medieval banquets, held twice every evening, at 6 and 9. These banquets are re-enactments— not altogether authentic, but certainly fun—of entertainments that could have taken place within the same walls some 500 years ago. As the guests file into the "great hall", lovely colleens in low-cut velvet gowns serve them mugs of mull wine; then everyone troops downstairs to the "main guard" for dinner. The menu varies, but usually consists of soup, half a capon, salad, vegetables and delicious homemade bread, topped off with rich dessert and washed down with plenty of mead (a potent distillate of apples and honey). Each diner gets a knife, and in true medieval style eats with his fingers. Meanwhile, handsome young players of both sexes sing old Irish airs, accompanying themselves on ancient instruments. The Bunratty Banquet costs £5.40, and reservations should be made in advance.

One branch of the many-branched River Lee, Cork City

The Treaty Stone and King John's Castle, Limerick

Beside the castle is the *Bunratty Folk Park,* containing characteristic farmhouses, fishermen's and laborers' cottages, and other features of the old, traditional Irish way of life. The Folk Park is open from 9:30 A.M. to 5:30 P.M. all year round, every day. Admission costs 40p.

The medieval banquets at Bunratty have proved so successful that, in 1967, a similar program was launched at *Knappogue Castle* in Quin, ten miles from Shannon Airport. These banquets, too, have attracted many visitors.

The most interesting sight in Ennis is *Ennis Abbey.* Completed in 1241, it was then rebuilt and added on to at frequent intervals into the 15th century, so that its details are a fascinating mixture of early and later styles. South of Ennis stand the ruins of two notable 12th century abbeys, *Clare Abbey* and *Killone Abbey,* both founded by Donal O'Brien, the last king of Munster.

To view the seascapes of West Clare and the Burren country, a visitor should drive west from Ennis to *Milltown Malbay*—hard by Spanish Point (where six ships of the Spanish Armada went down with all hands) and thence north to *Lahinch,* a popular resort town. From there, Route L54 runs west to the coast and over the five-mile-long *Cliffs of Moher,* which rise in sheer-walled majesty to 700 feet. These mighty seawalls are one of the finest sights in all Ireland. Seven miles further on is *Lisdoonvarna,* a small spa famous for its sulphur and magnesia springs and much frequented by courting couples on holiday.

From Lisdoonvarna, the main road winds north for 16 miles

through the Burren country of Ballyvaughan, on the shore of Galway Bay—and thence to Kinvara, in County Galway. *The Burren* is an amazing, almost waterless limestone wasteland, or karst, of which one of Cromwell's generals complained that it had "not a tree whereon to hang a man, no water in which to drown him, no soil in which to bury him." It is honeycombed by caves. The Burren is also remarkable for the abundance of certain rare plants, mostly of a distinctly southern or northern type. Strange to say, the Burren was thickly peopled in pre-historic times, and many dolmens and other prehistoric remains are to be found there.

County Galway is divided into two unequal parts by Lough Corrib and its outlet the River Corrib, at the mouth of which stands the old city of Galway. East Galway is mainly of interest to visitors because of its associations with W. B. Yeats and his circle. On the other hand, West Galway—better known as Con-nemara—is one of the foremost scenic attractions of Europe, a wild and beautiful land that continues to attract and enchant visitors from all over the world. And the rugged Aran Islands, in Galway Bay, are probably the most romantic spots ever.

Kinvara, on the road described just before that runs through the Burren, is the scene of a nightly banquet that resembles Bun-ratty's—and yet is quite different. Instead of a jolly blast, it is a restrained and exceedingly interesting "literary evening". Held in the restored keep of *Dunguaire* (pronounced "Dungooreh") *Castle,* guests sip Spanish wine and eat Galway Bay prawns while a fetching girl in medieval costume relates the fascinating legend of the castle. Then, upstairs in the banquet hall, they feast on a dinner featuring lobster cream soup and smoked salmon. At the meal's end, the young waiters and waitresses turn into excellent actors and actresses and present poems and excerpts from plays written during Ireland's literary revival in the early years of this century.

The literary banquet at Kinvara is held every night from May through September. It costs £5 for wines, dinner and entertain-ment. Reservations should definitely be made in advance.

Lovers of Yeats's poetry may want to stop at *Gort* (population 1,044) on the Limerick-Galway road. Just north of the town lies *Coole Park,* where the poet's great friend Lady Gregory lived; several Yeats poems evoke its woods and lakes. Four miles north-east of Gort stands *Ballylee Castle,* Yeats's "Thoor Ballylee". Yeats bought this tower and lived in it during the summers in the early 1920s. It figures prominently in his later work. The tower has been restored and is now a very interesting and well-arranged museum.

The city of **Galway** (population 27,726), picturesquely situated near the head of a noble bay, is the largest city in the West of Ireland, and that region's undisputed, if unofficial, capital. Yet it is far from typically Irish in appearance and atmosphere. For centuries, Galway traded extensively with Spain, and thus gradually came to acquire certain Spanish features, particularly in architecture and in the dress and manners of the people. Traces of Iberian influence are still found in Galway.

Historians have identified Galway with the city of Magnata (or Nagnata) mentioned by Ptolemy, but little is known about it before 1124, when local forces built a fort there. In 1232 Richard de Burgh took the city, which thereafter became a flourishing Anglo-Norman colony. Among its settler families were those which later came to be called the "Tribes of Galway" —the Blakes, Bodkins, Browns, D'Arcys, ffrenches, Kirwans, Joyces, Lynches, Martins, Morrisses and Skerrets. The Galway settlers kept the native Irish in their place: a 1518 bylaw declared that "neither O nor Mac shall strutte ne swagger thro' the streets of Galway". As recently as the late 18th century a Breton visitor, on announcing his intention to continue west into Gaelic-speaking Connemara, was greeted with gasps of horror and informed that the inhabitants there were "as savage as Iroquois".

Galway is small enough to be explored easily on foot. One obvious starting place is *Eyre Square,* a broad, open expanse next to the railway station and bus depot. (The Irish Tourist Office is just off it, in Victoria Place.) The entrance to the square is the Browne Doorway, a relic of Spanish architectural influence. Nearby are memorials to Liam Mellowes, a patriot of the 1916 uprising, and (in the form of a very appealing statue), to Padraig O Conaire (Patrick O'Connor), a famous Gaelic writer. But the monument most likely to affect Americans is the most recent one: a large bronze plaque set in a simple white stone slab that commemorates President John F. Kennedy's joyous visit to Galway on June 26–29, 1963, when he was made a freeman of the city.

On the corner of Galway's central Shop Street stands the only complete building left from the city's days of glory. Known as Lynch's Castle, it was built by a member of that prominent Galway family in the 14th century. It now houses a bank.

Another Lynch, or possibly the same one, founded Galway's lovely old *St. Nicholas' Collegiate Church,* on Lombard Street, in 1320. St. Nicholas' is unique among Irish churches for having a triple nave. Behind the church, on the site of the old jail, some words chiseled in stone over a gate recall a grim moment in Galway's history. In 1493, Mayor James Lynch Fitzstephen's son killed a young Spanish friend out of jealousy, whereupon the mayor, as town magistrate, condemned his son to death. But the young man was so well-loved that no one would carry out the sentence. To make sure that justice was done, the mayor, curbing his feelings as best he could, embraced the boy and then hanged him himself.

The year before this melancholy incident, according to legend, a Galway man named Rice de Culvy accompanied Columbus on his voyage of discovery to the New World. One story has it that Columbus, en route to America, put into Galway and prayed in St. Nicholas' for the success of his voyage!

The Spanish Parade, also called the Long Walk, is a promenade at the southwest corner of Galway; the Spanish Arch, which leads into it, survives from the old town walls. Across the River Corrib is **The Claddagh,** said to be the oldest fishing village in Ireland. This was the Irish town when the Normans held sway in Galway. The famous Claddagh gold ring, showing two hands clasping a heart, originated there. Beyond Claddagh, along Galway Bay, lies **Salthill,** one of the most popular seaside resorts in the country.

Upstream, a bridge crosses the river. When the salmon are running they can be seen from the bridge lying on the river bed in the thousands just below the weir. (The Corrib is the only entrance to the 1,200 square miles of Lough Corrib.)

Directly across the river from Galway proper rises the magnificent new Roman Catholic Cathedral of *Our Lady and St. Nicholas,* officially dedicated in 1965 by Cardinal Cushing of Boston. The main building is of Galway limestone and the flooring throughout of Connemara marble.

A considerably more ambitious trip over water is required to reach the **Aran Islands,** 30 miles out in Galway Bay. (These three arid, stony islands are, of course, the ones immortalized in J. M. Synge's *Riders to the Sea* and in Robert Flaherty's classic documentary film *Man of Aran.*) Two steamboats ply daily between Galway and the town of *Kilronan* on the largest island, *Inishmore* (population 864)—the C.I.E.'s **Naomh Eanna** and the Port and Liner services' *Galway Bay.* Round-trip tickets (good for one day) cost £3.70 and only half that price for children. Tickets are sold at the railway station (telephone, 2141) and at Kelly's Shipping Ltd., Commercial Docks (telephone, 2347), as well as at local travel agents. If possible, reserve in advance. Sailing times, depending on tides and weather, can be obtained from the operators or the Tourist Office.

The cruise, including a few hours of Inishmore, takes an entire day and is well worth it: many a traveler remembers it as the most interesting experience of his visit to Ireland. Especially on the smaller islands of *Inishmaan* and *Inisheer,* which can only be reached by curragh from Inishmore, Irish is still spoken freely, and the people still wear their traditional garb: long wool dresses for women, and, for men, homespun *bainin* jackets, heelless roughhide shoes called *pampooties,* and a many-colored woolen belt known as a *crios* (pronounced "criss").

Aer Arann operate daily flights between Galway and Inishmore. The plane holds ten people and flight time is 20 minutes. Round trip tickets cost £7.50 (about $15) and are available at Aer Arann, 1 Dominick Street, Galway (tel. 5119). If possible, reserve in advance.

At *Kilronan Pier,* cruise passengers are met by islanders offering to take them on jaunting car rides through Inishmore and out to Dun Aengus. These trips cost £4 officially, but certain drivers will negotiate. The ride is well worth the trouble. **Dun Aengus,** a low-walled circular fort 300 feet above the sea, is Ireland's most spectacular pre-historic ruin. One authority has called it "the most stupendous stone fort in Europe, perhaps the greatest military monument in the world, with walls eighteen to twenty feet thick, compared to some of which those of Mycene, the classic city of Agamemnon, are but insignificant".

The Number One event on the Galway calendar is Race Week, at the end of July and/or the beginning of August—three days of horse-racing at Ballybrit, two miles from town, accompanied by a great deal of drinking, dancing, singing and partying. The second biggest event is the colorful Oyster Festival, held around the third week in September, which ushers in the oyster-eating season with many a bang and nary a whimper.

Dublin's Bank of Ireland once housed Ireland's parliament

For many years, **Connemara,** the "wild west" of Galway, has been the joy and despair of generations of painters and writers who have striven in vain to capture its extraordinary magic in paint and words. Thackeray is typical. "The best guide-book that ever was written," he concluded, "cannot set the view before the mind's eye of the reader, and I won't attempt to pile up big words in place of those wild mountains, over which the clouds as they passed, or the sunshine as it went and came, cast every variety of tint, light and shadow; nor can it be expected that long, level sentences, however smooth and shining, can be made to pass as representations of those calm lakes by which we took our way. All one can do is to lay down the pen and ruminate, and cry, 'Beautiful!' once more; and to the reader say: 'Come and see!' "

The southern part of Connemara is studded with lakes, the northern part with mountains, notably the *Maamturks* and the *Twelve Bens* (or Twelve Pins). The region can easily be toured by bus or car. Towns and landmarks to look for include *Ballynahinch Lake and Castle;* **Clifden** (population 1,025), the delightful, "alpine" capital of Connemara; *Kylemore Abbey;* and, at Leenane, the awesomely narrow and step-walled fjord called *Killary Harbor. Oughterard,* on Lough Corrib, is Connemara's second most important town, and headquarters for salmon-fishers. To buy Connemara marble jewelry, the place to go is the Connemara Marble Products factory in Moycullen (8 miles from Galway); and for Aran sweaters and other homecrafted items, Standun's at Spiddal (10 miles from Galway, on the bay).

The long and much-indented coast of **County Mayo,** from Killary Harbor to Killala Bay, presents a succession of magnificent views—of sandy beaches, towering cliffs, rugged headlands and offshore islands, including Ireland's largest, Achill Island. Inland are moors and mountains, rivers and islet-studded lakes.

Southwest Mayo is much like Connemara. There are a number of places in this area that deserve a visit. *Cong,* where the famous Cross of Cong originated, is a pretty town between Lough Corrib and Lough Mask; the film *The Quiet Man* was shot there. *Delphi,* just north of Killary Harbor, is a place of indescribable beauty set in mountains. On Killary Harbor is a village with the longest placename in Ireland—Cooneenashkirroogohifrinn, meaning "the little harbor sliding to hell". And further north, on Clew Bay, is the charming fishing village of *Louisburgh.*

Guarding the mouth of Clew Bay is **Clare Island,** about 4,000 acres with a population of 160. In the 16th century Clare Island was the headquarters of one of the most colorful figures of Ireland's history, Grace O'Malley, sea-queen of the West. The sea-queen first married the ruler of Connemara, and after he died, Sir Richard Bourke, known as MacWilliam Oughter. According to tradition the marriage contract was for one year only, after which either party could dissolve the marriage simply by dismissing the other. Grace set to work garrisoning MacWilliam's castles with her own soldiers. When the year was up and her husband was entering Carrigahooley Castle, near Westport, Grace ended their alliance by shouting from within, "I dismiss you!".

Invited to London by Queen Elizabeth I, Grace showed little respect for that monarch's power. When Elizabeth offered to make her a countess, she haughtily replied that she, too, was a queen—Elizabeth's equal, not her inferior.

From the south shore of Clew Bay rises conical *Croagh Patrick* (2,500 feet). This is Ireland's holy mountain, hallowed by the memory of St. Patrick. In the year 441, he spent the 40 days of Lent on its lonely summit in prayer and fasting for the Irish people. Every year, on the last Sunday in July, thousands of devout Irishmen and Irishwomen climb Croagh Patrick to pray, some barefoot.

Further east, on an arm of Clew Bay, is **Westport** (population 2,947). Nearby is the spacious estate of the Marquess of Sligo, and on it the stateliest of all of Ireland's stately homes, *Westport House*. Originally built by an ancestor of the present marquess and the former's wife (a great-great-granddaughter of Grace O'Malley), the house was twice enlarged in the 18th century under the supervision of eminent architects. It contains family portraits, fine old English and Irish silver and several historical exhibits. Westport House is open to the public from April 1 to October 15, from 2 P.M. to 6 P.M. Admission to the house and grounds, which include a charming lake for boating and a Zoo Park is 80 pence for adults and half price for children.

About ten miles inland from Westport, one mile off the main road from Galway, Castlebar (the capital of Mayo), stands the beautiful old *Abbey of St. Patrick, Ballintubber*. Ballintubber Abbey is unique among Irish churches: it is the only one still in regular use that was founded by an Irish king, and the only one in which the Mass has been offered almost without a break for 750 years. Founded in 1216 by Cathal O'Conor, King of Connaught, it was already almost three centuries old when Columbus discovered America. Open to the public every day without charge, Ballintubber Abbey is known throughout the Catholic world as "the abbey that refused to die".

A few miles north of Westport is *Newport,* a picturesque resort on Clew Bay. From there, a road runs west to *Mallaranny,* where Mediterranean heather and fuchsia flourish in the remarkably mild climate. From Mullaranny the main road skirts the northern

Much of Connemara is bleak, poor—and beautiful

shore of Curraun Peninsula to where a bridge crosses Achill Sound to Achill Island.

Achill Island (36,248 acres) has three lofty mountains, and is almost entirely covered with heather. There are a surprising number of hamlets and small villages dotting the island. Notable among the bigger places are *Keel, Dooagh* and *Dugort*.

North Mayo boasts spectacular coastal scenery. The bleak and windswept **Mullet Peninsula** in the northwest affords glorious views of ocean, bay and islands; the center for exploring the peninsula is *Belmullet* (population 724). Mayo's north coast is also rugged and wild. In contrast, the county's largest town, **Ballina** (population 6,027), 39 miles east of Belmullet on the River Moy, is a quiet, peaceful place. In Ballina are the remains of an Augustinian friary built in 1427, and the Dolmen of the Four Maols, the tomb of four foster-brothers who murdered their tutor Ceallach in the 6th century, and were hanged by Ceallach's brother.

Ballina puts on a Salmon Festival every summer.

From Ballina, the coast road runs north into **County Sligo.** Packed into this relatively small county is a great variety of mountain, lake, and seacoast scenery. The *Ox Mountains,* in the southwest, form a backdrop to the coastal plain of western Sligo; north of Sligo town, steep-sided and flat-topped limestone hills dominate the landscape. The coast is mainly low-lying, but very scenic.

To a far greater extent than south Galway, Sligo is Yeats country. It was here that the poet summered, as a boy and a man.

It was here that he wrote his finest lyrics. And it was here that, in accordance with his wishes, he was buried.

Sligo town (population 14,080), the chief center of Ireland's northwest, is pleasantly situated between Lough Gill and Sligo Bay. Most of the town is on the south bank of the Garavogue River, which drains Lough Gill. Except on the seaward side, Sligo is surrounded by mountains at a few miles distance.

Being very compact, Sligo is easy to explore. The Irish Tourist Office is on Stephen Street, near the main shopping center. This is a good place to start a tour because the County Library nearby houses the very interesting *Sligo Museum*, which provides all kinds of useful archeological and historical background information including a special section on Yeats. The museum is open on Wednesdays and Saturdays from 3–5 P.M. During July, August and September, free walking tours, conducted by young students, set out from the Tourist Office every morning at 11. The 75-minute walk covers points of historical and cultural interest in the town. The guides should be tipped a minimum of 10p.

Of outstanding antiquarian interest is *Sligo Abbey*, on Abbey Street. It was founded for the Dominican Order by the Earl of Kildare in 1252, and rebuilt in 1404 after a fire. Its present ruined state dates from 1641, when Sligo was sacked by Sir Frederick Hamilton.

The oldest church in Sligo is *St. John's*, erected in the early 17th century. The fine *Catholic Cathedral*, next to it, was built between 1869 and 1874.

Lough Gill should certainly be explored. One of the best ways to do this is by motor launch, and during the summer season there are departures from Riverside, Sligo, each afternoon and evening. Full details are available from J. McCarrick (tel. 3791) who operates the service. Boats are available for hire on an individual basis through Peter J. Henry (tel. 2530). The lake rivals Killarney for natural beauty, and has historical interest, too. Among its wooded islands are *Cottage Island* and the larger *Church Island* (42 acres), containing the ruins of a church said to have been founded in the 6th century. Near the southeast shore of the lake is the tiny islet of *Innisfree*, immortalized in Yeats's celebrated lyric, "The Lake Isle of Innisfree".

The hills around Sligo abound in Stone Age, Bronze Age and early Iron Age monuments—cairns, dolmens, passage graves, gallery graves and ring forts. The free brochure *Prehistoric Sligo*, available at the Tourist Office, supplies details and maps showing their locations. The low hill *Carrowmore* contains the greatest concentration of megalithic remains in Ireland or Britain. And at the summit of imposing *Knocknarea* (1,078 feet) is a gigantic cairn known as Maeve's Mound, thought to be a monument to Queen Maeve of Connaught, who flourished in the first century.

On Monday afternoons, in summer, C.I.E. operates a 3½-hour Yeats Country Tour, which leaves the railway station at 2; cost is 80p. ($1.60). One stop, of course, is *Drumcliff*, 5 miles north of Sligo, with its ancient roadside cross. There in the little church-yard Yeats is buried, with flat-topped Benbulben ("Bare Ben Bulben's head") looming behind. A simple limestone slab bears the epitaph the poet composed for himself:

> *Cast a cold eye*
> *On life, on death,*
> *Horseman, pass by.*

A unique permanent memorial to the poet is the Yeats International Summer School, held annually in Sligo for two weeks in August. It provides lectures, seminars and discussions on Anglo-Irish literature, emphasizing the work of Yeats, but also dealing with other Irish writers, past and present. In the evenings there are poetry readings, films, and productions of Yeats' plays. Tuition fee is £30 for the session, but tourists passing through can attend any lecture for 40p. Inquiries should be addressed to Mrs. K. Moran, Secretary, Yeats International Summer School, Douglas Hyde Bridge, Sligo, Ireland.

The Fiddler of Dooney Competition, in which Ireland's champion fiddler is chosen, is held in Sligo in September.

County Leitrim, east of Sligo, and **County Roscommon,** east of Mayo and Galway, are off the beaten tourist track. Yet both hold rewards for the discerning visitor.

Strictly speaking, Leitrim is not an inland county, as it has 2½ miles of coast. The River Shannon forms its long eastern border. Lough Allen, an expansion of the Shannon, divides Leitrim almost completely in two: the land to the north is mountainous, while the southern portion is hilly, interspersed with lakes.

Leitrim's capital is **Carrick-on-Shannon** (population 1,497) in the south. The Shannon is navigable to a point just above the town. So Carrick-on-Shannon is the ideal place to begin a care-free, leisurely boat trip down Ireland's greatest river. You can rent a power launch there (consult the Tourist Board for opera-tors and prices), or, if you are feeling adventurous, join a large cruise in which you double as a member of the crew.

The Shannon also forms the eastern border of Roscommon. Much of this landlocked county is made up of level plain, bog-land and river meadow, broken by low hills and numerous lakes, for it forms part of Ireland's great Central Plain. **Boyle** (popula-tion 1,739) has a very distinctive Cistercian abbey founded in 1161. Lough Key Forest Park, four miles outside Boyle, is a pleasant mixture of woodland walks, interesting and rare trees, where the visitor gets a chance to see nature in a restful and informative setting. There are facilities for boating and a cafe which serves simple refreshments. And the town of **Roscommon** (population 1,600), the county capital, has a 13th-century Dominican abbey and a castle that was once one of the finest in all Ireland. The castle remains today a thoroughly impressive ruin.

County Donegal, at Ireland's northwest corner, is actually a part of the province of Ulster—the term sometimes used, inaccurately, to denote the six counties of Northern Ireland. With its long, dramatic and beautiful coast, its heather-hazed mountains (the "hanging hills of Donegal"), deep glens and many lakes, Donegal is rightly famous for its scenery. (Significantly, the official *Illustrated Ireland Guide* devotes more space to Donegal than to any other county, except Cork, the largest.)

To enter Northern Ireland from Donegal, a visitor has to head for the border crossing between Lifford (Donegal's administrative capital) and Strabane, south of Derry (or Londonderry). At Donegal town, route T18 bends inland, and runs through miles of wilderness with occasional villages, to the customs stations. The coastal route, T72, is much longer—225 miles if the traveler rounds all headlands and inlets—but it is much more scenic.

Lonely **Lough Derg,** in southern Donegal, is the scene of Ireland's most important pilgrimage. Legend tells how St. Patrick spent 40 days of prayer and fasting on a small island in the lake to rid it of evil spirits. (The island is now called *Station Island.*) No one knows when the pilgrimages began, but during the Middle Ages men of high rank came to Lough Derg from Christian Europe. The pilgrimage continued to flourish, even during the penal times, and flourishes today. During the season, June 1 to August 15, only pilgrims are allowed on the island. A pilgrimage lasts three days, during each of which only one meal—of dry bread and black tea—is allowed.

Donegal town (population 1,458), at the head of Donegal Bay, is a pleasant, thriving market town. The fishing center of **Killybegs** (population 1,085), 17 miles west of Donegal, is also a center for the manufacture of much-prized Donegal carpets. *Kilcar,* a picturesque village 8 miles further west, is a center for Donegal handwoven tweed. Embroidery, knitting and other cottage industries also flourish in the vicinity. **Ardara** (population 547), further north on the bays of Loghros More and Loghros Beg, is also an important center for homespun tweeds.

Letterkenny (population 4,329), the largest town in Donegal, overlooks fjord-like Lough Swilly. The mountainous area between Lough Swilly and Lough Foyle, the *Inishowen Peninsula,* tapers toward **Malin Head,** the most northerly point in Ireland. And east of Lough Foyle, Northern Ireland begins.

Perhaps more than any other Irish county, Donegal casts a spell over visitors—calling them back for another visit.

CHAPTER 7

THE MIDLANDS AND THE BOYNE VALLEY

Between Carlow in the south, and Cavan and Monaghan in the north, lie five other inland counties—Laois, Kildare, Offaly, Westmeath and Longford—which, together with Roscommon and east Galway, occupy Ireland's Central Plain, and make up the region called the Midlands. Broken in places by low hills, the generally limestone Central Plain is extensively covered with glacial deposits of clay and sand. It has considerable areas of bog and numerous lakes.

Lacking the scenic splendors of the South, West and North, the Midlands attract comparatively few visitors from abroad—except anglers and sportsmen, who flock there for the good fishing and hunting. Yet there is much there to interest the visitor willing to stray from the tourist track.

County Carlow, the second smallest county in Ireland after County Louth, lies wedged between the uplands of Counties Wexford and Kilkenny. In its capital, **Carlow** (population 9,588), on the River Barrow, stand the ruins of 13th-century *Carlow Castle.* At *Browne's Hill,* 2 miles to the east, is a notable dolmen; its capstone, the largest in Ireland, is believed to weigh 100 tons.

Seven miles south of Carlow, on the Barrow, stands the ruins of *Black Castle,* erected in 1181. Further south, two miles east of Muine Bheag, are the very substantial remains of *Ballymoon Castle,* with curious and interesting architectural features.

County Kildare is the least hilly county in all Ireland. Large tracts of its west and northwest are occupied by the extensive *Bog of Allen.* The center of the county is the beautiful unen-

A typical cottage in Co. Donegal

closed plain of the **Curragh,** the scene of Ireland's greatest horseraces. Kildare is preeminently shooting and hunting country—and it is next door to Dublin.

But the county has its share of historical relics, too. **Naas** (population 4,023) is the site of the royal palace of the ancient kings of Leinster. **Maynooth** (population 1,753), Ireland's chief center for training priests, has *Carton House,* an imposing mansion in the classic style, designed by Richard Castle about 1740, and the longtime residence of the Dukes of Leinster.

Kildare town (population 2,561) has *St. Brigid's Cathedral,* incorporating part of a 13th-century structure, and a round tower 105 feet tall.

County Kildare's best-known institution is the *National Stud* at Tully, the property of the Irish government, which has produced many, many famous race horses. On the grounds are the charming Japanese Gardens, open to the public, which portray, with Oriental symbolism, the vicissitudes of man's existence.

Except for the *Slieve Bloom Mountains* on its northwest border and some lesser hills in its southeast section, **County Laois** is low-lying, and in places quite flat.

Port Laois (population 3,133), its main town, was once called Maryborough. In the 16th century it was fortified as part of a plan to crush the O'Mores, chiefs of the district. Of these fortifications, only the outer wall of the tower remains. Four miles east of the town is the prominent *Rock of Dunamase.* On its summit are the ruins of a great castle, once a fortress of Dermot MacMurrough, king of Leinster, and later an O'More stronghold. For centuries, this castle was the scene of many battles, until Cromwell's troops dismantled it in 1650.

At **Killeshin,** near the Carlow border, the doorway of the ancient church is a particularly fine example of Irish-Romanesque art. *Mountmellick,* seven miles north of Port Laois, was founded by Quakers. Four miles northwest of it, in the pretty village of *Rosenallis,* is the oldest Quaker burial ground in Ireland.

Until recently, **Portarlington** (population 3,117) had a French Huguenot colony. Today, the town's most conspicuous feature is the cooling tower of Portarlington Power Station—the first of several electricity-generating plants which burn Ireland's ubiquitous native fuel, peat. The fuel is produced by machinery from about 120,000 tons of turf annually, collected from the 4,000-acre Clonsast Bog, four miles north of the town.

At *Castletown* village, south of *Mountrath* (population 1,051), the women still practice such ancient handcrafts as basket-making, rug-making and leather-working.

County Offaly lies at the very center of Ireland. It is largely level plain and bogland. Its most famous feature is Clonmacnoise, beside the Shannon, one of the most important concentrations of ruins in the country.

Tullamore (population 6,809), the county capital, is the busy market center of a fertile farming district. North of the town, on the Durrow Abbey estate, is the site of the celebrated *Monastery of Durrow,* founded by St. Colmcille. The famous *Book of Durrow,* now at Trinity College, Dublin, was written here in the 7th century. Except for the high cross, few traces of the monastery remain.

Clonmacnois, on the River Shannon four miles north of the village of Shannonbridge, is one of Ireland's most celebrated holy places. In 584 St. Ciaran founded a monastery there which became the most famous of all the monastic centers in the land. The city of learning flourished under the patronage of successive kings, including Rory O'Conor, the last high king, who was buried there in 1196. But it was also the object of raids by native chiefs, Danes and Anglo-Normans. In 1552, a thousand years after it was founded, it was despoiled by the English garrison at Athlone, and a century later Cromwell's soldiers completed the destruction.

The site contains a cathedral, eight ruined churches, two round towers, three sculptured high crosses and parts of two others, over

200 monumental slabs and the remains of a castle. So extensive are the Clonmacnoise remains that descriptions of the more important ones take up three pages of the *Illustrated Ireland Guide*.

County Westmeath is famous for its many lakes, several of which contain trout in abundance. Island-studded *Lough Ree,* an expansion of the Shannon in the west, is the largest lake in the Midlands. Near its shores is the "Goldsmith country", where landmarks familiar to readers of that poet's *The Deserted Village* may be seen.

Mullingar (population 6,790), the county capital, is the center of a famous cattle-raising area. Its most important building is the Catholic Cathedral of Christ the King, an imposing Renaissance-style structure with twin 140-foot towers that was dedicated in 1939 by the late Cardinal Glennon of St. Louis. The cathedral's spacious interior contains much beautiful decorative work.

Athlone (population 9,825), on the Shannon, is the "capital" of the Midlands, as Galway is of the West. It is a busy road and rail junction and an important harbor for inland navigation. Athlone has been the scene of many battles because of its strategic location. In 1001 Brian Boru marched on the town while his fleet sailed up the Shannon. Two centuries later Anglo-Normans occupied Athlone and built a castle there to guard the crossing. In 1257 the first town walls were erected.

Over the next centuries possession of the town was often disputed. Queen Elizabeth I made Athlone the seat of the Presidency of Connacht. Cromwell's Court of Claims, dealing with the lands of the dispossessed Irish, was housed in the castle.

Directly overlooking the bridge at Athlone stands *King John's Castle,* a strongly fortified building dating back to the 13th century. In it are the governor's apartments. Fragments of the old town walls can be seen near *St. Mary's Church* (Church of Ireland), the old tower of which is said to contain a bell taken from Clonmacnoise in 1552.

Athlone was the birthplace of the celebrated tenor John McCormack.

County Longford, another quiet, lake-studded inland area, is perhaps chiefly notable for its associations with Goldsmith and with the novelist and essayist Maria Edgeworth (1767–1849). It was also the scene of the crucial Battle of Ballinamuck in 1798, in which the British General Lake defeated a combined French and Irish force under the French General Humbert culminating the hopes for Irish independence that year.

Edgeworthstown (population 624), on the Dublin-Sligo road, has a long association with the Edgeworth family, who settled there in 1583. Their family residence, *Edgeworth House,* still stands. Notable visitors to it in the 19th century included William Wordsworth and Sir Walter Scott, whose *Waverley Novels* were influenced by Maria Edgeworth's writings.

County Cavan, the southernmost of the nine counties of Ulster, lies on the edge of the Central Plain; in its northwest it rises to *Cuilcagh Mountain* (2,188 feet), on the southern slope of which is the source of Ireland's greatest river, the Shannon. The River Erne, rising in Lough Gowna and flowing north, spreads itself out in myriad small sheets of water separated by promontories and islands. These and other of Cavan's small lakes are very beautiful, and much favored by anglers.

The county's chief town, **Cavan** (population 3,208), was in ancient times the seat of the O'Reillys, rulers of East Breifne. *Shantemon Hill,* 3 miles northeast, was the O'Reillys' inauguration place. Northwest of Cavan town is the fine demesne of Farnham House. Beyond Farnham, on an island in Lough Oughter, is the O'Reilly 13th century fortress, *Cloughoughter Castle.* This castle remained the O'Reillys' until the English Plantation of Ulster early in the 17th century; then, after being retaken by Colonel Myles O'Reilly in 1641, it was seized by Cromwell's men in 1653 and systematically despoiled.

Killinkere, six miles southwest of Bailieborough, is said to be the birthplace of General Philip Sheridan of Civil War fame. And it was from little Ballyjamesduff, near Virginia, that there emigrated to America in 1789 one William James—the grandfather of William James, the philosopher, and Henry James, the novelist.

County Monaghan, like Cavan and Donegal, is remarkable for its great number of little hills. Like Cavan, it is dotted with pretty lakes, which afford excellent fishing. It is sometimes known as the MacMahon country after the powerful family that long dominated the area.

The capital, **Monaghan** (population 5,256), is a thriving agricultural center that shows little evidence of its antiquity.

Carickmacross (population 2,100), an old town with a wide main street in the southern part of the county, is the home of Carick-macross lace. This exquisite fabric earned the town a great name in the past; it is still produced there in small quantities.

The Boyne Valley. The River Boyne (70 miles) is only the fifth longest in Ireland—after the Shannon, the Barrow, the Suir and the Blackwater—but it is the most fabled. Its valley is a place of memories, and nowhere can the history of Ireland—traced by its monuments—be better studied. Among its numerous historic places are **Tara,** the seat of the high kings of Ireland; the **Hill of Slane,** where St. Patrick lit the Paschal fire; and the prehistoric royal tumuli of **Brugh-na-Boinne.** The Battle of the Boyne was fought on the banks of the river, in 1690—when William of Orange defeated James II in that decisive victory.

The Boyne glides through County Meath on the northeast fringe of the Central Plain and forms, in its final stage, the southern border of County Louth. Both Meath and Louth are particularly rich historically. For this reason—and because both have seacoasts—they will be treated separately from the counties of the Midlands.

County Meath consists almost entirely of rich limestone plain, with occasional low hills. It was for centuries a separate province, which included Westmeath, ruled by the pagan and early Christian kings of Ireland. For this reason the county is often called "Royal Meath".

Trim (population 1,700), on the Boyne, is one of the oldest ecclesiastical centers in Ireland. Although little remains of the ancient settlements, Trim and the country around it are full of interesting ruins, mostly dating from the Middle Ages. *Trim Castle* is the largest Anglo-Norman fortress in the country; it was originally built, in the 12th century, by Hugh de Lacy. The town has two lesser fortresses, *Nangle's Castle* and *Talbot's Castle,* the latter built in 1415 by the then Lord Lieutenant of Ireland, Sir John Talbot. This castle was later converted into a school, in which Arthur Wellesley, who was to become the Duke of Wellington, received his early education. Trim's most conspicuous ruin, the Yellow Steeple, opposite Trim Castle, was originally a part of 13th-century St. Mary's Abbey, destroyed by fire in 1368.

At **Newton Trim,** half a mile west of Trim, are the remains of the 13th-century Abbey of Sts. Peter and Paul—founded in 1206 by Simon de Rochfort, the first Anglo-Norman bishop of Meath. At *Laracor,* two miles south of Trim, Dean Swift preached; the house of his beloved "Stella" (Esther Johnson) still stands there. *Dangan Castle,* 1½ miles further south, was the residence of the Duke of Wellington's family, the Wellesleys.

Tiny **Clonard,** near Kinnegad, offers no hint of its glorious past. Yet it was there that St. Finian, in the 6th century, founded a monastic school that was to become renowned throughout western Europe. From it came such famous leaders and teachers as St. Brendan and St. Colmcille.

The ancient town of **Kells** (Irish:*Ceanannus Mor;* population

2,391) reached importance after St. Colmcille founded a monastery there in the 6th century. Kells has several remarkable old structures, among them high-roofed (38 feet) *St. Colmcille's House,* with stone walls almost four feet thick. An especially perfect, though topless, round tower stands nearby; near it rise several fine old high crosses. The monastery of Kells was, of course, the source of the celebrated Book of Kells at Trinity College, Dublin.

Navan (Irish: *An Uaimh;* population 4,605), at the confluence of the Blackwater and the Boyne, is the largest town in Meath. While Navan itself contains little to interest the visitor, the surrounding countryside does. *Athlumney Castle,* 1½ miles to the south, is a striking 16th century ruin with a notable souterrain, or underground passages and chambers. The extensive ruins of 12th century *Bective Abbey,* 5 miles south of Navan, should also be seen.

On the other hand, the Hill of Tara, 6 miles south of Navan, is likely to disappoint the visitor who goes there unprepared. This royal acropolis was, in ancient times, nothing less than the political and cultural capital of Ireland. The scene of a great triennial *feis,* or national assembly, at which laws were enacted and revised and tribal disputes settled. Old manuscripts tell of a banquet hall at Tara seven hundred feet long and ninety wide. Yet apart from the reputed coronation-stone of the high kings, and some low mounds and earthworks, there are few traces of Tara's past grandeur.

Another historic hill, further down the Boyne Valley, rises a mile north of the pretty village of *Slane* (population 483). Atop **Slane Hill** St. Patrick, in 433, kindled the Paschal fire to proclaim Christianity throughout the land. The remains of a 16th century church, on the site of the church and monastic school he founded there, still stand.

Brugh-na-Boinne, a few miles to the east, is a remarkable pre-Christian burial ground of kings. It is made up of Bronze Age tumuli, the three principal ones are about a mile apart—at Knowth, Newgrange and Dowth. The last two have been opened and explored: they consist of entrance passages and curiously constructed burial chambers. Electric light has been installed in the Newgrange tumulus for the benefit of visitors. There is a small museum at the site.

Further down the Boyne Valley, where the river separates Meath from County Louth, is where the Battle of the Boyne was fought. And at the village of *Fourknocks,* 5 miles west of Balbriggan, County Dublin, is an impressive prehistoric site. The decorated uprights and lintels of the tumuli there resemble those at Newgrange. The site dates from about 1800 B.C.

Only 317 square miles, **County Louth** is the smallest in Ireland; but like Rhode Island in the United States, it makes up for its diminutive size with scenic diversity and historical interests. Between the River Boyne on the south and Carlingford Lough on the north Louth consists of fertile, undulating country with a seacoast of sandy beaches and occasional rocky headlands; in the north is the mountainous and highly scenic Cooley Peninsula. This territory figures prominently in the epic tales of ancient Ireland. It was the haunt, notably, of Cuchulainn, hero of the legendary Red Branch Knights at the beginning of the Christian era. It has also figured prominently in Ireland's history, numerous relics of which are to be found within its boundaries.

On the Mattock River, a tributary of the Boyne, stand the remains of the first Cistercian house in Ireland, *Mellifont Abbey*. It was built in 1142, on land granted by Donough O'Carroll, king of Oriel. Its first abbot was trained at Clairvaux, in France, by St. Bernard. In 1172, Henry II received the submissions of O'Neill and other northern chiefs at Mellifont. Of the surviving buildings, the most interesting are the abbey church, the chapter house and the lavabo. The latter a curious structure, originally octagonal, where the monks washed their hands before meals.

Still more impressive are the remains of the ancient monastic settlement of *Monasterboice,* founded by St. Buithe, a native of the place, probably toward the end of the 6th century. These ecclesiastical remains are among the most important in western Europe. Surrounded by an old graveyard, they consist of two churches, a round tower, three sculptured crosses, two early grave-slabs and a sundial.

On the Boyne, four miles west of the Irish Sea, is the city of **Drogheda** (population 19,762), an industrial center and seaport

Off the beaten track—Leighlin Bridge, Co. Carlow

with a harbor on the Boyne estuary. Drogheda is an ancient and historic town. Established as a fortified settlement by the Danes in 911, it came to rank with Dublin and Wexford as a trading center. Under the Anglo-Normans, who walled the town, Drogheda became, by the 14th century, one of Ireland's four principal towns. In 1394 Richard II held court there to receive the submissions of the Irish Princes of Leinster and Ulster.

During the 15th and 16th centuries, Drogheda continued to prosper, but in the 17th century the town sustained some heavy blows. In 1641 Phelim O'Neill attempted to capture it and was repelled. Eight years later Cromwell took Drogheda by storm, and butchered 2,000 soldiers and townspeople. Many of the survivors were shipped off to the West Indies.

In 1689 Drogheda declared for James II, but surrendered to the victorious William after the Battle of the Boyne. In the 18th and 19th centuries the town declined considerably. With the growth of industry in recent times, however, it has regained much of its past importance.

Of the town's original ten gates, only *St. Lawrence's Gate* survives. It is one of the most perfect specimens in Ireland. The ruins of the 13th-century Augustinian Abbey of *St. Mary d'Urso* consist of a central tower with a fine pointed arch spanning Abbey Lane. The abbey occupied the site of an earlier foundation associated with St. Patrick and St. Columba. The *Magdalen* steeple, a lofty two-story tower, is all that remains of a Dominican priory founded in 1224 by the archbishop of Armagh.

A much later archbishop of Armagh is commemorated in Gothic-style *St. Peter's Church,* in which is enshrined the head of the Blessed Oliver Plunket, martyred at Tyburn, in London, in 1681.

The Tholsel, a fine, square building surmounted by a cupola, is now a bank.

On the south side of the city, in County Meath, is a large mound called *Millmount.* It is said to have been erected over the grave of a son of Milesius who died in 1029 B.C. A 14th-century fort atop the mound was stormed by Cromwell in 1649. Millmount Fort was garrisoned by the British until recent times: after the 1916 uprising it served as a temporary prison, and it was shelled during the Civil War (the Troubles) following the Anglo-Irish Treaty.

Dundalk (population 21,672), at the head of broad Dundalk Bay, is the largest center and capital of County Louth. This old city has witnessed many important events in Irish history—especially during the centuries when it was a frontier town of the English Pale and subjected to frequent raids by the O'Neills. Today few traces of its active, colorful past remain.

CHAPTER 8

Northern Ireland, the Six Counties, or Ulster . . . by whatever name, the British enclave at Ireland's northeast corner is a fair and friendly land that Americans too often bypass. A visitor cannot really say he has seen Ireland unless he ventures north of the border as well as south of it. That border, after all, has only existed since 1921; before then, the region witnessed some of the greatest (and most tragic) events of Irish history, from which the whole country's history is inseparable. Northern Ireland's historical links with the United States, incidentally, are stronger than America's ties with any territory of comparable size. No fewer than six Presidents—Jackson, Polk, Buchanan, Arthur, McKinley and Wilson were descended on both sides, and seven others on one side, from Ulstermen.

While the Republic is overwhelmingly Catholic, Northern Ireland is predominantly—by a 2 to 1 ratio—Protestant. The economy of the first is mainly agricultural and that of the second is mainly industrial. Northern Ireland is famous for the great ships turned out by the shipyards of Belfast. It is famous as the home of fine Irish linen and for its delightfully varied landscape: its lakes (including Ireland's largest, Lough Neagh), its mountains (including the fabled Mountains of Mourne) and, above all, its incomparable coast, the most salient feature of which is the geological marvel, the Giant's Causeway.

The city of **Belfast** (population 360,000), on the River Lagan where it enters Belfast Lough, is Ireland's chief industrial center and seaport. It is the second largest city in all Ireland. And it is the seat of Northern Ireland's government.

Although it is of quite recent growth, Belfast has a long

history. A fort stood on the site in ancient times, and in the late Middle Ages, the village that grew up around it was alternately in the hands of the English and the O'Neills. Early in the 17th century the English uprooted the native inhabitants, planting their lands with Protestant settlers from Devonshire and Scotland. After 1685, Huguenot refugees introduced improved methods of linen-weaving which stimulated Belfast's trade. But by 1700 the town's population was still only about 2000.

In the 18th century Belfast grew—slowly but steadily. In 1791 two steps were taken in Belfast that were to bear important consequences. Wolfe Tone and several friends founded the United Irish Society, whose agitation for Irish independence was to lead to the abortive uprising of 1798. And two brothers, William and Hugh Ritchie, began to build ships on the River Lagan.

The Belfast of today is almost wholly the product of the Industrial Revolution: the application of mechanization to linen-weaving and shipbuilding during the 19th century enormously increased the city's commerce and caused its population to surge from 25,000 to 300,000. Today, more than one in ten of all Irishmen, and close to one in three inhabitants of Northern Ireland, lives there.

Belfast is big and busy, but even its most civic-minded citizens would hesitate to call it beautiful; it looks, in fact, exactly like what it is—a vast, sprawling monument to the age of the railway, the steam ship and the mechanized loom. Yet like Manchester, Birmingham and other British cities that burgeoned from small beginnings during the same period, Belfast undeniably possesses a certain gray, grim and gritty grandeur. And for the visitor who shares the poet John Betjeman's fondness for Victorian and Edwardian architecture and decoration, Belfast can be a source of endless delight.

A visitor's first stop in Belfast should be the Northern Ireland Tourist Board office in River House, 48 High Street. There he can pick up free copies of various descriptive booklets, a calendar of events in Northern Ireland, brochures on the Folk and Transport Museums near Belfast, a list of recommended fishing sites in Northern Ireland and handouts covering the city and provincial guided bus tours.

A few steps from the tourist office is a wide intersection called Castle Place, after which a broad thoroughfare called Donegall Place leads south to Donegall Square and the City Hall. In Donegall Square, tickets to the guided city tours (run by Belfast Corporation Transport) can be obtained at an information kiosk (telephone 21661). However, such tours are not available during periods of hostility or tension.

Provincial bus tours are still available and are handled by Ulsterbus Ltd., Great Victoria Bus Station. Tours of the lovely country around Belfast cost as little as 45 pence ($1). Full day trips range as far as Donegal and Dublin. Details and reservations can be obtained at the Bus Station, or by telephoning 44791.

Belfast's single most imposing building is the *City Hall*, a handsome Renaissance-style structure of Portland stone, in the center of Donegall Square. In front of it stands a statue of Queen Victoria, who appears to be averting her eyes from the distasteful spectacle of onrushing traffic in Donegall Place. On the west side of the domed City Hall are a *Great War Memorial* and a *Garden of Remembrance*, and on the east side is a sculptured group commemorating the victims of the *Titanic* disaster in 1912. The *Titanic* was built in Belfast. The largest and fastest luxury liner of her time, she struck an iceberg on her maiden voyage to New York and sank with a loss of more than 1,500 lives.

The Linenhall Library, on Donegall Square North, contains a fine collection of books of general and historical interest.

Three hundred yards west of the City Hall is the *College of Technology*, attended by 10,000 students. Next to it is the *Royal Belfast Academical Institution*, formerly Belfast College, which numbered among its pupils Lord Kelvin, the great inventor, and Lord Bryce, the noted statesman and scholar.

Queen's University, in the southern suburbs of Belfast, is open to the public on weekdays from 9:30 to 4:30 and on Saturdays from 10 to 12. Adjoining it are the 38-acre *Botanic Gardens*, well worth a visit for those interested in rare flowers and plants. The *Ulster Museum and Art Gallery*, in the Gardens, contains interesting exhibits—particularly a growing collection of modern art. Here, too, are portraits of all 13 U. S. Presidents of Scottish-Irish ancestry. Open weekdays, 9–6.

The *Ulster Transport Museum*, on Witham Street, covers 200 years of Irish transportation. It is heartily recommended to visitors with children in tow. The museum is open Monday through Saturday from 9–6. Admission is 15p. for adults, and 5p. for children.

The *Ulster Folk Museum*, eight miles from the city center on the road to Bangor, is situated in a beautifully kept park. Its exhibits provide a very complete picture of what life in the North of Ireland was like prior to the coming of the Industrial Age. A completely enchanting place, with real cats licking real

Castle Coole, home of the Earl of Belmore

cream in real cottages, it makes history in another sense as well—
it is open on Sundays!

About five miles from the city center, in Stormont Park near
the village of Dundonald, stands the imposing *Parliament Building,* which housed Northern Ireland's bicameral legislature
(Commons and Senate) and will be the site of whatever official
regional assembly is decided upon for the area.

Another strongly-recommended side trip from Belfast is that
to Carrickfergus, ten miles north on Belfast Lough (see below,
under "Antrim").

County Antrim, which takes in the greater part of Belfast, forms
the northeast corner of Ireland; the promontory known as **Torr
Head,** on the North Channel, is only 13 miles from Scotland.
Most of the country is a hilly plateau that drops sharply to the
sea on the east and north, but its western portion consists of
Lough Neagh and the fertile valley of the River Bann. On the
east a fine coast road runs north from Larne, curving around
headlands between which the beautiful Glens of Antrim open
to the sea. On the north coast is Antrim's (and Ireland's) most
famous natural curiosity, the Giant's Causeway.

According to some medieval writers, the town of **Carrickfergus**
(population 15,000) was named after Fergus Mac Erc, who
became the first Irish king of Scotland. It is chiefly notable for its
remarkable castle, *Carrickfergus Castle,* built at some time
between 1180 and the early 13th century, either by John de

Courcy, the first Anglo-Norman invader of Ulster, or by Hugh de Lacy, who succeeded him. It was probably the first real castle erected in Ireland, and is certainly one of the largest and best preserved in the country. It stands by Carrickfergus harbor on a rocky peninsula. The castle's portcullis, with its ancient machinery, still exists; inside the curtain walls are an outer and inner courtyard giving on to a massive rectangular keep, 58 feet by 56 feet and 80 feet high. The lowest of the keep's five stories contains the castle well and a dungeon.

Carrickfergus Castle was captured in 1305 by Robert the Bruce, but in 1318 was retaken by the English, who retained it for the next 300 years. During the English Civil War it changed hands more than once. The castle and town, held in 1688 for James II, were taken the following year by the Williamite general Schomberg. In 1690 King William landed there to launch his succesful campaign against King James and his followers. John Paul Jones sailed into Belfast Lough in the American ship *Ranger* in 1778; just off Carrickfergus he defeated the British ship *Drake*, whose captain was killed in the encounter.

Also worthy of note in Carrickfergus are the *Church of St. Nicholas,* part of its chancel dates from 1305–6; the *North Gate,* a part of the old town walls; and the Town Hall, recently remodeled from the old *County Antrim Courthouse,* erected about 1613. Near the North Gate there once stood an inn operated by the ancestors of Andrew Jackson, whose parents emigrated from Carrickfergus in 1765, two years before the future President was born.

Larne (population 18,200), 14 miles north of Carrickfergus, is notable for two quite different reasons. To tourists, it offers the

Belfast City Hall

shortest ferry route from Britain—from Stranraer, in Scotland. To archeologists, it offers a wealth of information about the earliest known inhabitants of Ireland: from the Curran, a long, tapering gravel spit 10 to 20 feet above high water, have been unearthed thousands of flint flakes and implements from the Neolithic Period.

But Larne is notable, too, as the "gateway" to the Antrim Glens. It is from there that the Antrim Coast Road winds 25 miles north of Cushendall passing the nine celebrated Glens of Antrim and a succession of basalt and limestone cliffs and headlands.

In *Glenballyemon,* the glen that extends inland from the attractive little town of Cushendall, a great many Stone Age axes and other implements have been found. From Cushendall, the road runs north to Cushendun, where numerous flint tools have been found embedded in the bank of the River Dun in distinct layers. The main road to the next coastal town, Ballycastle, runs overland; but a far more picturesque, though tortuous, road runs along the majestic cliffs that guard Ireland's extreme northeast corner.

Ballycastle (population 3,000), a market town and seaside resort, is the logical starting point for a visit to Fair Head and/or Rathlin Island. *Fair Head,* six miles to the east, is Ireland's northeast extremity; its 636-foot summit affords a glorious view of the adjoining coast, Rathlin Island and the Scottish coast and islands. *Rathlin Island,* ravaged by Norse raiders in 790, was the scene of three memorable massacres, one by the Scottish clan Campbell and two by the English; its cliff-girt shores are reached by a 6-mile boat trip from Ballycastle.

But Rathlin Island plays hard to get. Stormy tides separate it from the mainland and the tourist can find himself overstaying his leave. The helicopter has been a modern boon to the islanders—100 hardy farmers and fishermen—sometimes, in winter, cut off for weeks.

Moira O'Neill, the gentle poetess of the Glens, has a view of Rathlin that the tourist should heed:

> There's Raghery Island beyont in the bay,
> And the dear knows what they be doing out there,
> But fishing and fighting and tearing away,
> And who's to fault them, and what do they care?

A visit to Rathlin Island is for the adventurous. They will gain in courage, as did Robert the Bruce, when in a cave on Rathlin he saw the spider try, try and try again.

Thirteen miles west of Ballycastle, along Antrim's north coast, is the wonderful rock formation known as the **Giant's Causeway.** One of the world's outstanding geological curiosities, the Causeway was formed by the cooling of lava which burst through the earth's crust in the Cenozoic Period between the Antrim coast and the Isle of Skye off Scotland. At the Antrim end this cooling resulted in the splitting of the basaltic rock into innumerable prismatic columns, mostly hexagonal but some pentagonal and others with seven or more sides.

Three miles south of the Causeway is the little town of **Bushmills,** known to anglers for the salmon- and trout-fishing in the River Bush. Perhaps more widely known though for the Irish whiskey that is distilled there.

Portrush (population 5,000), eight miles west of the Giant's Causeway by the County Londonderry border, is one of the most popular seaside resorts in Northern Ireland. It has beautiful, truly golden beaches—which the local people think quite ordinary and a golf course which has been the scene of many a championship match.

The valley of the River Bann, which runs through much of western Antrim, is pretty country, but its towns contain little to interest visitors. The town of **Antrim** (population 7,300), however, is interesting for its situation at the northeast corner of Lough Neagh. Lough Neagh, 17 miles long and 11 wide, covering 153 square miles, is far and away the largest lake in Ireland and Great Britain. It is ringed by Counties Antrim, Londonderry, Tyrone, Armagh and Down.

County Down, south of Antrim, is one of the most fertile counties in Ireland. It is remarkable for its many low hills. In striking contrast are the massive granite Mountains of Mourne in the south, with Slieve Donard rising from the sea to a height of 2,796 feet. In the east, long and island-studded Strangford Lough is almost completely enclosed by the Ards Peninsula. Down's long, beautiful and varied coastline is dotted with popular resorts.

That part of Belfast east of the River Lagan is in County Down. From it, a good road—and a rail line—run northeast by Belfast Lough, past Holywood, to **Bangor** (population 35,000). One of the largest and best-equipped seaside resorts in Ireland, Bangor is otherwise chiefly of interest for its early history—though few traces remain. The town began its existence about 555, when St. Comgall founded a monastery there. The monastery became one of the most celebrated of Ireland's monastic schools, attracting students from Britain and the Continent. One of Bangor's missionary sons was St. Columbanus, who went to Gaul as a missionary, founded three monasteries and died there in 615; another was St. Gall, the apostle of Switzerland, who founded the monastery that became the nucleus of the town and canton named for him. The monastery at Bangor was destroyed by the Danes in 824. After much subsequent rebuilding and renewed destruction its stones were used in 1617 for a new

Protestant church on the site. The church is still called the *Abbey Church*.

The coast road from Bangor to Donaghadee passes the old-world village of Groomsport, where King William's advance army landed in 1689. **Donaghadee** (population 3,700) is another seaside resort, and a good base for touring the Ards Peninsula. Keats spent a holiday here and might have lived longer if he had stayed. Kipling, Wordsworth, Tennyson and even Byron visited County Down, but poetry didn't mix too well with fried eggs and bacon, and rugged living left little time for composing lyrical passages.

Across the peninsula, at the head of Strangford Lough, is **Newtownards** (population 15,300). The town's orderly layout of streets intersecting at right angles, unusual in Ireland, originated in the early 17th century when Protestants were settled on the confiscated lands of Con O'Neill. Just east of Newtownards are the ruins of 15th-century *Movilla Abbey,* on the site of a famous monastery and school founded in the 6th century by St. Finian. South of Newtownards is Strangford Lough, the greatest migratory bird sanctuary in the British Isles.

Downpatrick (population 3,878), a quiet market town, is built on hilly ground by the marshy valley of the River Quoile. A place of note since earliest times, Downpatrick is the administrative center of the county named after it. In 432, St. Patrick landed at Saul, 2 miles northeast, to begin his mission in Ireland. It was at Downpatrick that he died, many years later, on ground granted him by his first Irish convert, the chief Dichu. A large granite boulder, outside the *Downpatrick Cathedral* (Church of Ireland), inscribed with a cross and the name PATRIC, was placed there in modern times to mark the saint's reputed grave. There is no proof, however, that the Anglo-Norman conqueror John de Courcy actually did collect the bones of saints Patrick, Brigid and Colmcille and deposit them in the cathedral when it was dedicated to St. Patrick. De Courcy made Downpatrick his headquarters and added the saint's name to the original *Dun* (fort). *Inch Abbey,* three miles downstream from Downpatrick, was also founded by him in 1180. The ruins are quite extensive.

Newcastle (population 4,600) is beautifully situated on Dundrum Bay at the foot of Slieve Donard. *The Mountains of Mourne* extend southwestward from there for about 15 miles. Tours of the Mourne district begin and end at Newcastle.

Warrenpoint (population 4,200), a pleasant town with wide, tree-lined streets, occupies a fine situation on land jutting out from the north shore of Carlingford Lough, opposite County Louth. About 1½ miles above Warrenpoint stand the ruins of *Narrow Water Castle,* of Norman origin. Across the narrow water from this picturesque ruin lies the Republic—and it's anybody's guess how much picturesque contraband goes to and fro!

Newry (population 11,400) is a sizable port and industrial center, important from early on because of its situation at the "Gap of the North", the main pass through the uplands separating Ulster from Dublin and the south. Its most interesting building is *St. Patrick's Church* (Church of Ireland), originally constructed in the 16th century, which is said to have been the first Protestant church built in Ireland.

Like Down on the east and Monaghan on the south, landlocked **County Armagh** has many gentle hills—mainly in the south. In the north is a rich fruit-growing area which has earned Armagh the title of "the Garden of Ulster". Portadown and Lurgan are important linen-weaving centers. In recent years the county has been recognized as one of the best rose-growing areas in the world.

Armagh was the scene of many events in the epic literature of ancient Ireland. The ancient city of Armagh, the early seat of the kings of Ulster, has been the ecclesiastical capital of Ireland for more than 1500 years.

The county derives its name from the town of **Armagh** (population 12,300). The name itself comes from *Ard Macha* (Macha's Height); presumably referring to the warrior Queen Macha. About the year 300 she constructed a great fort, as her royal residence, west of the hill on which the town later grew (see below). The cathedral city dates from 443, when St. Patrick established his primatial see on the hill Ard Macha, granted him by a local chieftain named Daire. St. Patrick also founded a monastic school there that became a great center of learning.

In successive Danish invasions Armagh was repeatedly destroyed, and then rebuilt. In 1004 King Brian Boru visited the town and presented 20 ounces of gold to the church; ten years later he and his son Murrough were buried there, slain during their great victory over the Danes at Clontarf. Between 1014 and 1170, Armagh reached its greatest brilliance, and in 1169 Rory O'Connor, the last high king of Ireland, founded a professorship at Armagh "for all the Irish and the Scots." In 1566 the town was demolished by Shane O'Neill to prevent it from being occupied by the English, and in 1642 the rebuilt town was again destroyed, by Phelim O'Neill.

Armagh's two cathedrals, Catholic and Protestant, face each other on hilltops. Many of the well-laid-out streets have marble pavements. In the town are many fine houses of the Georgian and Regency periods, and much elegant wrought-iron work.

The Church of Ireland cathedral occupies the traditional site of the church built by St. Patrick. In its present form it is mainly

Giant's Causeway, a formation of geometric rock columns, Co. Antrim

the result of restoration work done in the 18th and 19th centuries. Outside the north transept is a tablet marking the supposed site of Brian Boru's grave. Inside the cathedral are numerous monuments to English and Irish noblemen and the effigies of former archbishops.

The newer Catholic cathedral, erected between 1840 and 1873, in decorated Gothic style, has a fine west front with twin spires. Its interior is richly decorated, the walls being entirely covered with mosaics, including medallions of the saints of Ireland. The red hats of the cardinal archbishops of Armagh hang in the cathedral. The archbishop's residence adjoins the cathedral, and the diocesan college is close by.

At the northern end of the pleasant green called the Mall stands the attractive *Courthouse.* The *Royal School* nearby was founded in 1627 by Charles I. Across the road from it is the *Observatory,* established in 1791. The *County Museum,* on the east side of the Mall, contains, among other displays, a fine collection of bronze weapons and implements.

The Palace of the Protestant archbishop, built in the late 18th century, stands in spacious grounds on Dobbin Street. Its chapel is particularly fine. On the grounds are the ruins of a Franciscan friary founded in 1266.

Two miles west of Armagh is a great elliptical earthwork enclosing a huge mound thought to be the burial mound, or tumulus, of Queen Macha. The site is called *Eamhain Macha,* or Macha's Fort. For 600 years, down to 332, Eamhain was the seat of the kings of Ulster; in the first century, under King Conor Mac Nessa, it was the headquarters and training school of the legendary Red Branch knights, whose chivalry and daring are celebrated in many an ancient Irish epic.

The village of **Tynan,** 8 miles west of Armagh, is noted for its ancient crosses. The village cross is 13½ feet high, and there are three other high crosses on the grounds of *Tynan Abbey*.

Portadown (population 22,000) is a busy industrial center. Its nurseries have won an international reputation for their roses. Eight miles northwest, where the River Blackwater enters Lough Neagh, is the village of *Maghery,* a headquarters for fishermen. On the road between Portadown and Maghery is the one-time home of the father of the Confederate general "Stonewall" Jackson.

Lurgan (population 24,000) is an important linen-weaving center. It was founded early in the 17th century by Protestant settlers, destroyed by Phelim O'Neill in 1641, rebuilt in 1661, destroyed by King James's forces in 1689, and finally, after James's defeat, restored again. In an effort to decongest the Belfast area, Lurgan and Portadown are merging to form the new "lineal city" of Craigavon. New industries are moving in, housing, schools and hospitals are gradually being built to attract residents, as are recreational facilities such as a marina and an artificial ski slope!

County Londonderry—called Derry south of the border and by many Nationalists in the county, too—lies on Ireland's north coast between Antrim on the east and Donegal, in the Republic, on the west. It is named for the city of Londonderry, Northern Ireland's second largest city, at the county's western edge. Except for the coastal plain in the north and the Bann Valley and lowlands bordering Lough Neagh in the east, the county is hilly, rising to the Sperrin Mountains in the south along the Tyrone border.

The city of **Londonderry,** or Derry (population 52,000), stands on a hill at a bend in the River Foyle, upstream from Lough Foyle. It dates from the foundation of a monastery there by St. Colmcille (St. Columba) in 546. ("Derry" is the anglicized form of the Irish *Doire,* meaning oak grove.) As other churches were built there, the town of *Doire Colmcille* (St. Columba's Oak Grove) became a place of increasing importance. Although the Anglo-Normans never invaded it, Derry was frequently the prey of marauders, by sea and land.

Not until 1600 did the English gain a permanent foothold, when Sir Henry Docwra landed and took the town, fortifying it with stones obtained by pulling down the churches. In May of 1608 the young chieftain of Inishowen, Cahir O'Doherty, burned the town. Two months later he was defeated and killed, and his lands confiscated, along with those of the O'Neills and O'Donnells. King James I then granted more than 20,000 acres of the confiscated lands to the city of London, whereupon the name Londonderry began. A large colony of Protestants was planted there, and by 1618 the walls fortifying the town were completed.

In 1649 Sir Charles Coote, then holding the town for Cromwell, reached an agreement with Owen Roe O'Neill; at Coote's request O'Neill brought an army there and helped him to lift a four-month Royalist siege. But Londonderry's most famous siege took place in 1689. The garrison and inhabitants (including many Protestants who had fled there from other parts of Ulster) were besieged for 105 days by forces loyal to James II. The besiegers threw a boom across the river, downstream from the town, which barred the way to provision ships. Thousands of Londonderry citizens died of starvation and disease; the survivors found their chief inspiration in a heroic clergyman, the Reverend George Walker. At last, on July 28, an English convoy forced the boom and relieved the town.

Today, the city walls that were never breached still stand in a ring around the old city, while the new city sprawls outward in all directions—including a section on the opposite (east) bank of the Foyle. The center of the old town is a square called the Diamond, atop a hill; from it, Shipquay Street—said to be the steepest business street in Ireland or Great Britain—descends to Shipquay Gate. Almost opposite this opening in the city wall is the *Guildhall,* on Shipquay Place, a modern Gothic building completed in 1912. Among the Londonderry Corporation's treasures on display there are a sword said to have belonged to Cahir O'Doherty and the mayor's chain and medal of office, presented to the city by William III.

Off Bishop Street, which runs off the Diamond opposite Shipquay Street, is the *Protestant Cathedral of St. Columb,* erected in 1628–33, a fine example of the simple, harmonious style known as "Planter's Gothic." In the vestibule is a cannonball which fell in the churchyard during the siege; wrapped around it was a paper outlining terms of surrender, but the garrison's reply was a defiant rejection. Many relics of the siege are housed in the cathedral's chapter house.

Near St. Columb's, at the head of Bishop Street, is *Bishop's Gate,* a triumphal archway erected in 1789 in place of the old gate. The old walls are now laid out as a promenade; on them are many of the cannons used in the great siege, including the largest of all, "Roaring Meg".

The *Catholic Church of St. Columb,* outside the walls on Long Tower Street, occupies the site of the ancient *Teampall Mór* (Great Church) erected in 1164 by the first bishop of Derry. Outside it is a stone on which, according to tradition, St. Colmcille customarily knelt to pray.

The Catholic cathedral *(St. Eugene's),* at the head of Great James Street, is a well-proportioned Gothic-style building with a handsome spire.

Limavady (population 5,500), 17 miles east of Londonderry, dates from the Plantation of Ulster. It was there that Miss Jane Ross, in 1851, heard an itinerant fiddler play the hauntingly beautiful Irish melody now known all over the world as the "Londonderry Air", and noted down the music.

Coleraine (population 15,000) stands on the estuary of the River Bann. It is said to have been named *Cúil Rathain* (Ferny Corner) by St. Patrick.

Portstewart (population 5,000) is a seaside resort much favored by British visitors.

In the central and southern parts of County Londonderry are many lovely glens and rugged mountains, as well as interesting prehistoric and historic sites. The latter are mainly around *Garvagh, Maghera* (the birthplace of Charles Thomson, secretary of the first U. S. Congress, who wrote out the Declaration of Independence), and *Dungiven* (the site of a 12th-century Augustinian priory, of ruined 17th-century fortifications, and of ancient Banagher Church—three miles distant).

Derrymore House, Britain's only "stately home" with a thatched roof

One of the most beautiful of Ireland's inland counties, **County Tyrone** offers a great diversity of scenery—mountains and hills, glens and river valleys, moors and little plains and some of the best fishing in Ulster. As the ancient patrimony of the O'Neills, Tyrone was for centuries the rallying ground of resistance to the invader.

The O'Neills' chief seat was at **Dungannon** (population 7,500), in eastern Tyrone, not far from Lough Neagh. From there they constantly warred on the English until the 17th century.

Two and a half miles south of **Cookstown** (population 6,600) is *Tullaghoge Fort,* in ancient times the residence of the O'Hagans, who, as justiciars of *Tir Eoghain,* performed the solemn inaugurations of the O'Neill chiefs. The last such ceremony was the inauguration of Hugh O'Neill in 1593. In 1602 the Elizabethan general Mountjoy destroyed the inauguration stone.

Omagh (population 12,000), the capital of Tyrone, is pleasingly situated in a wide valley among foothills of the Sperrin Mountains. Its principal buildings are the twin-spired Catholic church, the Church of Ireland, and the Courthouse. Omagh is a convenient base for exploring the exceptionally lovely countryside all around, on foot or bicycle or by car.

Strabane (population 9,300), situated on the River Mourne near where it unites with the Finn (from Donegal) to form the River Foyle, is the main "gateway" to Donegal. A bridge over the Foyle connects Strabane with Lifford in Donegal. The town was the birthplace, in 1747, of John Dunlap, who went to Philadelphia and in 1771 started the *Pennsylvania Packet,* America's first daily newspaper. Later, Dunlap printed the Declaration of Independence, and during the Revolution subscribed £4,000—a huge sum in those days—to Washington's cause. He learned his trade at Gray's printing shop in Strabane, which still exists there.

The largest permanent American exhibit in the British Isles, Mellon Folk Park, will open in 1976 near Strabane, and will feature a reconstruction of a colonial village, an Indian settlement, and an American colonial museum.

The most remarkable feature of **County Fermanagh** is the River Erne, which meanders through it in a northwesterly direction from County Cavan, broadening out into island-strewn expansions called Upper and Lower Lough Erne. While there are narrow strips of lowland along the river and lakes, the rest of the county is hilly. Fermanagh is known as the "Lakeland of Ulster".

Enniskillen (population 6,318), the capital of the county, is charmingly situated on an island in the river that joins the two lakes. In ancient times it was a stronghold of the Maguires, rulers of Fermanagh, whose confiscated lands were granted early in the 17th century to Sir William Cole. The town was then settled by English families. In 1689 Enniskillen was one of the main Anglo-Scottish strongholds in Ulster, and James's attacking forces were more than once repulsed.

Only a turreted gateway now remains of Enniskillen Castle. The Church of Ireland cathedral in Enniskillen retains a part of its 17th-century tower. The Catholic church is a fine modern Gothic structure.

Portora Royal School, west of the town, was founded by James I in 1618. Oscar Wilde was once a pupil there. Nearby is the ruin of Portora Castle, built by Sir William Cole.

Devenish, an island in Lower Lough Erne two miles northwest of Enniskillen, is famous for its fine ecclesiastical remains—on the site of a monastery founded there by St. Molaise in the 6th century. The most remarkable structure there is the 82-foot round tower, one of the most perfect in Ireland. *Teampall Mór,* the Great Church, 80 feet long and 25 wide, is in ruins, but there is a deeply splayed round-headed door in the south wall. Nearby is a tomb of the Maguires. Further up the hill is the most recent building, *St. Mary's Abbey,* probably erected, on the evidence of a Latin inscription in the rock, in 1449. South of it stands an unusual high cross, with the crucifixion carved on its east face.

On White Island and on Inishmacsaint, north of Devenish in the lake, stand the ruins of two more ancient churches. The islands can be reached by boat from the village of Killadeas, 8 miles north of Enniskillen. At *Killadeas Church* are some curiously carved stones thought to date from the 7th or 8th centuries.

Just beyond the point at which Lower Lough Erne narrows to a river is the town of *Belleek,* on the Donegal border. Belleek is famous for its lustrous chinaware.

Upper Lough Erne is a veritable maze of waterways spreading around countless islands and headlands. The area can be viewed by car from Enniskillen by taking the Belturbet (south) road, turning left to cross the lake via the bridge spanning Trasna Island, and then turning north along the eastern shore.

The *caves of Fermanagh,* in the limestone hills in the western part of the county, extend underground in fascinating labyrinths: except for County Clare, this is the most interesting area to speleologists in Ireland. Fermanagh's best-known cave system is the one called *Marble Arch.* It is 3½ miles west of Florence Court, where the Cladagh River issues from a complex system of large caves and galleries, parts of which can only be explored by boat.

CHAPTER 9

FACT FINDER

Accommodations available in Ireland range from luxury hotels to farmhouses. Since a visit is considerably affected by accommodation conditions, the two Irish governments do their best to insure that proprietors maintain their premises in accordance with strict standards of cleanliness and comfort. To this end both governments make frequent unannounced inspections and also set ceilings on the prices of rooms in various categories. The Irish are a friendly and traditionally hospitable people; they are also well aware of the importance of tourism to their national economies. For all these reasons a visitor can be pretty confident of receiving fair value for his money.

Both the Irish Tourist Board (Bord Failte) and the Northern Ireland Tourist Board annually issue lists of all government-approved accommodations, the former in two brochures, *Official Guide to Hotels, Guesthouses, Holiday Camps and Hostels* and *Town and Country Homes/Farmhouses*. The Northern Ireland Tourist Board also publishes *Northern Ireland: All the Places to Stay*, another reliable guide. All three publications provide complete information about the places listed, and anyone planning to stay in Ireland for any length of time should certainly get hold of copies, either from the Stateside tourist offices nearest his home, or on his arrival in the country. They can often be great savers of time, money and patience.

All establishments are graded in six categories. Grade A* indicates de luxe hotels of top quality, and Grade A hotels or guest houses of a very high standard of comfort and service. Grade B* hotels and grade B guest houses are well furnished and offer comfortable accommodation. Establishments in Grade C also provide comfortable accommodation but offer fewer amenities, while Grade D denotes premises that are clean and comfortable but possess limited facilities.

The following table conveys an approximate idea of prices for a double room, including breakfast for two persons. (Here, the word "approximate" should certainly be stressed: a visitor who stops at towns that are off the beaten tourist track is very likely to find excellent accommodations at a considerably lower price than those given below.)

Symbol and Grade		Minimum Price	Maximum Price
***1	A*	£14 ($28)	£18 ($36)
***	A	£ 8 ($16)	£15 ($30)
**	B*&B	£ 7 ($14)	£12 ($24)
*	B&C	£ 5 ($10)	£ 9 ($18)
*	D	£ 4 ($ 8)	£ 7 ($14)

As noted in an earlier chapter, Irish guest houses are invariably less expensive than Irish hotels—and very often newer and cleaner as well.

Food in Ireland tends to be plain and hardy. If you're an expert on French cuisine, you may find the Irish kitchen badly wanting. But if you're a meat-and-potatoes diner, you will be satisfied. Restaurant prices vary widely, from almost incredible lows in villages to moderate prices in large cities. You can get a good meal for anywhere from £1.50 to £5.

On the pages that follow are a selection of recommended Irish hotels and guest houses, restaurants, pubs and shops. Because of space limitations only a few of the many worthy establishments in these categories can be listed. For the same reason, only those cities and towns are covered where a visitor would be most likely to stop. Persons seeking further information about accommodations are again referred to the government's publications.

In the accommodations listings below, the abbreviation "p.b." preceded by a numeral, indicates the number of rooms with private baths in the given hotel or guest house. Almost all the establishments listed are ready to provide visitors with full board and reduced rates for a stay of three days or longer; and most offer sizable reductions for children.

THE REPUBLIC OF IRELAND

Aran Islands Co. Galway (pop. 1,496)

GUEST HOUSES: Inishmore, *Johnston Hernon's Kilmurvey House*. 10 rooms. May 1–Sept. 30. Inishere, *Greigmore House*. 6 rooms. *Sean O Congaile* (An Siopa), 6 rooms. Both May 1–Sept. 30.

Athlone Co. Westmeath (pop. 9,824)

HOTELS: ***Prince of Wales*, Church Street, 49 rooms, 6 p.b.; ***Royal*, 45 rooms, 7 p.b.; **Shamrock Lounge*, 34 rooms, 8 p.b.; **The Hodson Bay*, Lakeview, 27 rooms, 18 p.b.

RESTAURANTS: The restaurants of the first three hotels listed above all give good value.

Bundoran Co. Donegal (pop. 1,326)

HOTELS: ***1 The Great Southern*, 106 rooms, 69 p.b. ***Central*, 29 rooms, 5 p.b. **Hamilton*, 30 rooms, 8 p.b.

GUEST HOUSES: *Casa del Monte*, 6 rooms. *Rossmore*, West End. 15 rooms.

RESTAURANT: *The Great Southern Hotel Restaurant*. Plainly furnished, offering a palatable and nourishing Franco-Irish cuisine at reasonable prices.

Cashel Co. Tipperary (pop. 2,679)

HOTELS: ***Cashel Palace*, 20 rooms, 20 p.b. **Grant's Castle*, Main Street, 14 rooms, 2 p.b.

RESTAURANT: *Cashel Palace Hotel Restaurant*. Notable for the beauty and charm of its location, in a former archbishop's palace.

Clifden Co. Galway (pop. 1,025)
HOTELS: ***Alcock and Brown*, 20 rooms, 20 p.b. **Clifden Bay*, 45 rooms, 25 p.b. **Abbeyglen House*, 18 rooms, 16 p.b. Easter–Sept. 30. *Rock Glen Country House*. 11 rooms. Easter–Oct. 1.

MOTEL: *The Connemara Inn*. 15 rooms, 15 p.b. April 1–Sept. 30.

GUEST HOUSES: *Lavelle's*. 11 rooms. *Corrig Cuan*. 5 rooms. April–Sept.

Clonmel Co. Tipperary (pop. 11,600)

HOTELS: ***Clonmel Arms*, Sarsfield Street, 41 rooms, 20 p.b. ***Minella*, 40 rooms, 37 p.b. **Hearn's*, Parnell St. 31 rooms, 15 p.b. *County*, 10 rooms.

Cong Co. Mayo (pop. 233)

HOTEL: ***1 Ashford Castle*. 77 rooms, 77 p.b. A medieval cum 19th century castle, luxuriously renovated and admirably situated on Lough Corrib.

Cork Co. Cork (pop. 129,000)

HOTELS: ***1 The Imperial*, South Mall. 83 rooms, 83 p.b. ***1 Jury's*, Western Road. 96 rooms, 96 p.b. ***1 Metropole*, MacCurtain Street. 132 rooms, 80 p.b. ***Silver Springs Hotel*, Tivoli. 72 rooms, 72 p.b. **Victoria*, Patrick Street. 77 rooms, 16 p.b. **Corrigans*, MacCurtain Street. 20 rooms. **Glengarriffe*, Orchard Road. 12 rooms, 2 p.b. *Vienna Woods*, 16 rooms, 6 p.b.

MOTEL: *Cork Airport Motel*, Kinsale Road. 20 rooms, 20 p.b.

GUEST HOUSES: *Glenvera*, Wellington Road. 30 rooms. *Ashford House*, Donovan's Road. 6 rooms. *Laurels*, Western Road. 10 rooms. *St. Kilda's*, Western Road. 6 rooms.

RESTAURANTS: *Arbutus Lodge Hotel* offers classical French cuisine. Expensive, but considered the best in Cork. *The Oyster Tavern*, Market Lane. One of the finest restaurants in the South of Ireland. *Imperial Hotel Restaurant*,

South Mall. A fine, solid, old-fashioned place. *Jury's Hotel Restaurant*, Western Road. New, with very well-cooked fare. *Cactus Chinese Restaurant, The Green Door*, and *The Leprechaun*, at Nos. 23a, 92 and 101 Patrick Street, respectively. Inexpensive nourishment. *Mackesy's*, 74 Oliver Plunkett Street, off the Grand Parade. Meat and fish dishes, masculine atmosphere, budget prices. *Blackrock Castle*, good but expensive French cooking.

PUBS, MUSIC, THEATER: See Chapter 5, under Cork.

USEFUL ADDRESSES: *Irish Tourist Office*, Monument Buildings, Grand Parade; *General Post Office*, Oliver Plunkett Street, open daily except Sunday 8–6:30. *CIE bus station* at Parnell Place, one block from Patricks Bridge. Shops close on Wednesdays at 1 P.M.

Dublin Co. Dublin (pop. 750,000)

HOTELS: ***1** Gresham*, O'Connell Street. 220 rooms, 185 p.b.; ***1** Jury's*, Ballsbridge. 314 rooms, 314 p.b.; ***1** Royal Hibernian*, 48 Dawson Street. 93 rooms, 93 p.b.; ***1** Shelbourne*, St. Stephen's Green. 166 rooms, 166 p.b.; ****Tara Tower*, Merrion Road. 84 rooms, 84 p.b.; ****Clarence*, 6 Wellington Quay, 70 rooms, 32 p.b.; ****Green Isle*, Naas Rd. 56 rooms, 56 p.b.; ****Montrose*, Stillorgan Rd. 190 rooms, 160 p.b.; ***Highfield*, 1 Highfield Rd. 12 rooms, 4 p.b.; ***Holyrood*, 29 Harcourt St. 29 rooms, 9 p.b.; ***Lansdowne*, Pembroke Road, Ballsbridge. 27 rooms, 13 p.b.; ***Ormond*, Upper Ormond Quay. 76 rooms, 18 p.b.; **Adelphi*, 68 Lower Gardiner Street. 16 rooms, 4 p.b.; **New Moran*, Talbot St. 50 rooms; **Ormsby*, Eccles St. 32 rooms, 22 p.b.

GUEST HOUSES: **Mount Herbert*, 7 Herbert Road, Ballsbridge. 57 rooms, 39 p.b.; **Elgin*, 23 Elgin Road, Ballsbridge (opposite U.S. embassy). 7 rooms. **Montrose House*, 16 Pembroke Park. 8 rooms.

RESTAURANTS: *Snaffles Restaurant*, 47 Lower Leeson Street. First-class French cuisine. *Chopstick Restaurant*, 60–61 Dame Street. Chinese food; inexpensive. *Gresham Hotel: Tain Grill* is good and inexpensive; *Huntsman Grill* is somewhat more expensive but very good eating; *Gandon Room* is hotel's main dining room with menu based on French cuisine. *Jury's Hotel: Embassy Restaurant and Martello Roof Restaurant*, Ballsbridge. Two top-flight dining rooms, the second commanding a fine view of Dublin. *Kilimanjaro*, 142 Lower Baggot Street. Simple and reasonably-priced. *The Lord Edward*, 23 Christchurch Place. Noted for its sea food. *Royal Hibernian Hotel*, Dawson Street: *Lafayette Restaurant*. Very stylish, excellently-prepared food; *Rotisserie* is a very good, medium priced grill; *Bianconi* has lower priced but hearty fare. *The Golden Orient*, Lower Leeson St. Fine and inexpensive Indian food with, downstairs; *Tandoori Rooms*, one of the best eating places in Dublin. *The Bailey*, Duke Street. Good seafood and atmosphere. *The Country Shop*, 23 St. Stephen's Green. Delicious, traditional Irish food. Cuisine for weightwatchers.

PUBS, MUSIC, THEATER, MUSEUMS: See Chapter 4.

SHOPPING: *Aran sweaters:* Clery's, O'Connell Street; *Irish linen:* same; *Carrickmacross lace:*

Brown Thomas, Grafton Street; *Irish family crests:* Heraldic House, Upper O'Connell Street; *Irish phonograph records:* Mc-Cullough-Pigott, 11 Suffolk Street; *Waterford crystal and glass:* all shops (prices are fixed throughout Ireland).

USEFUL Addresses: *The Central Dublin Tourism Office* is at 51 Dawson Street, the *CIE booking office* at 59 O'Connell Street, the *General Post Office* at the center of O'Connell Street (open 8 A.M. to 11 P.M. daily). *The American Embassy* is in Ballsbridge. *Irish Tourist Board*, Baggot St. Bridge.

Ennis Co. Clare (pop. 6,000)

HOTELS: ***Old Ground,* O'Connell Street. 55 rooms, 55 p.b.; **Queen's,* 27 rooms.

RESTAURANT: *Old Ground Hotel Restaurant.* Well-cooked and well-served food.

Galway Co. Galway (op. 28,000)

HOTELS: ***1 Great Southern,* Eyre Square. 128 rooms, 121 p.b.; ***Ardilaun House,* Taylors Hill. 53 rooms, 43 p.b.; **Imperial,* Eyre Square. 67 rooms, 43 p.b.; **Odeon,* Eyre Square. 64 rooms, 31 p.b.; *American,* Eyre Square. 19 rooms, 2 p.b.

GUEST HOUSE: *Ardeen,* Rockbarton North. 6 rooms, 1 p.b. Note: there are a great many good hotels and guest houses in the adjacent bayside resort of Salthill.

RESTAURANTS: *The Claddagh Room Restaurant, Great Southern Hotel*, Eyre Square. First-class fare amid surroundings of quiet elegance. *Ardilaun House Hotel Restaurant,* Taylors Hill. Pleasant atmosphere and good food; medium prices. *Lydon's,*

5 Shop Street. Busy and very inexpensive.

PUB: *The Galway Oyster,* Eglinton Street is Galway's newest and choicest pub.

SHOPPING: *Aran sweaters:* Standun's in Spiddal, 11 miles west of Galway City. *Claddagh rings:* all jewelers' shops. *Connemara marble jewelry:* the Connemara Marble Products factory at Moycullen, 7 miles northwest of Galway City.

USEFUL ADDRESSES: *The Irish Tourist Office* is just off Eyre Square, one block east. *The General Post Office* (open 9–6:30 weekdays and 9–10:30 A.M. Sundays) is on Eglinton Street. The *CIE train station* and *bus depot* are on Eyre Square. Shops close at 1 P.M. Thursdays.

Glengarriff Co. Cork (pop. 244)

HOTEL AND RESTAURANT: ***Casey's,* 18 rooms, 5 p.b. The dining room is bright and pleasant, and the fare dependably good.

Howth Co. Dublin
(pop. included under Dublin)

RESTAURANTS: *The Abbey Tavern.* No visit to Ireland is complete without a visit to this world-famous "singing tavern." *The King Citric.* Possibly Ireland's best seafood restaurant.

Kenmare Co. Kerry (pop. 1,046)

HOTEL AND RESTAURANT: ***1 The Great Southern Hotel,* 59 rooms, 44 p.b. This secluded hotel, on the glorious "Ring of Kerry," has just about everything a traveler could wish for. The dining room serves good, nourishing fare and commands a magnificent view of Kenmare Bay.

Kilkenny Co. Kilkenny (pop. 10,000)

HOTEL: ***Newpark, Castlecomer Road. 45 rooms, 35 p.b.
RESTAURANTS: Kyteler's Inn, center of town. Fine food, well served, in agreeable medieval surroundings. Newpark Hotel has excellent food.

Killarney Co. Kerry (pop. 7,184)

HOTELS: ***1 Dunloe Castle, Beaufort. 140 rooms, 140 p.b.; April 1–Oct. 31. ***1 Europe. 168 rooms, 168 p.b., ***1 Great Southern, 181 rooms, 181 p.b.; ***Three Lakes. 76 rooms, 70 p.b.; **Dromhall, Muckross Road. 63 rooms, 12 p.b.; **Glen Eagle, 56 rooms, 33 p.b.; **Grand, Main Street. 30 rooms, 3 p.b.

MOTEL: The Killarney Ryan, Dublin Road. 168 rooms, 168 p.b.

GUEST HOUSES: Castle Lodge, Muckross Rd. 12 rooms. *Linden House, New Road. 10 rooms, 6 p.b.

RESTAURANT: Hotel Europe Restaurant. Light and spacious, with a great view of sea and mountains. Fine cooking.

Kinsale Co. Cork (pop. 1,622)

HOTELS: ***Acton's. 61 rooms, 39 p.b. ***Trident, Worlds' End. 40 rooms, 40 p.b.

RESTAURANTS: The restaurants of both Acton's and the Trident serve good, plain fare. Try also Gino's, Le Bistro or The Vintage.

Limerick Co. Limerick (pop. 57,000)

HOTELS: ***1 Jury's, Ennis Road. 96 rooms, 96 p.b.; ***Cruise's, O'Connell Street. 81 rooms, 55 p.b.; ***Hanratty's, Glenworth St. 43 rooms, 28 p.b. **The Limerick Ryan, Ennis Road. 184 rooms, 184 p.b.; **Shannon Arms, Henry Street. 20 rooms, 1 p.b.

MOTEL: Parkway, Dublin Road. 103 rooms, 103 p.b.

GUEST HOUSES: *Alexandra House, 5 Alexandra Terrace. 13 rooms. *Ballineen, Ennis Road. 5 rooms. *St. Rita's, Ennis Road. 5 rooms.

RESTAURANTS: The Brazenhead Grill, O'Connell Street. A very modern cellar restaurant. Good steaks. Jury's Hotel Restaurant, Ennis Road. Smart and modern.

SHOPPING: Genuine Limerick lace: the Good Shepherd Convent, Clare Street, opposite the People's Park.

USEFUL ADDRESSES: The Irish Tourist Office is at 62 O'Connell Street. The General Post Office, open weekdays 9–6:30 and closed Sundays, is on Lower Cecil Street, off O'Connell Street. The CIE train and bus station is on the southeast edge of town. Shops close at 1 P.M. on Thursdays.

Newmarket-on-Fergus Co. Clare (village) (pop. 1,000)

HOTEL AND RESTAURANT: ***1 Dromoland Castle, 67 rooms, 67 p.b., April 1–Oct. 31. This romantic castle, set ·in 1,500 acres of lawns, woods and lakes, is surely one of the most luxurious hotels anywhere. The restaurant is very splendid, and so is the food. Eight miles from Shannon Airport.

Newport Co. Mayo (village) (pop. 420)

HOTEL AND RESTAURANT: ***Newport House, 30 rooms, 22 p.b. April 30–Sept. 30. The restaurant in this attractive Georgian house features both English and French cooking.

Parknasilla Co. Kerry (location)

HOTEL: ***1 The Great South-

ern Hotel, 75 rooms, 57 p.b., April 1–Oct. 31.

Shannon Airport Co. Clare

HOTEL: ***Shannon Interna-tional*, 126 rooms, 126 p.b.

RESTAURANTS: *Airport Restau-rant.* First-rate French and Irish cuisine. *Shannon International Hotel Restaurant.* Only lunch is served, but snacks are available in the evening. A very well-run establishment, with Irish cooking.

SHOPPING: *The Shannon Airport Duty-Free Shop* has bargains ga-lore in just about every kind of Irish merchandise.

Sligo Co. Sligo (pop. 14,080)

HOTELS: ***Great Southern.* 58 rooms, 27 p.b.; ***Ballincar House.* 18 rooms, 14 p.b. ***Jury's.* 60 rooms, 60 p.b. **The Silver Swan.* 24 rooms, 12 p.b. **Imperial.* 41 rooms, 1 p.b. *Cen-tral.* 11 rooms.

GUEST HOUSE: *Fatima*, John Street. 7 rooms.

RESTAURANTS: *Bonne Chère*, Market Street. Congenial atmos-phere; expensive. *Ritz Cafe*, O'Connell Street, and *Savoy*, High Street, offer good plain cooking at low prices.

USEFUL ADDRESSES: The *Irish Tourist Office* is one block east of the bridge at 14 Stephen Street. The *CIE train* and *bus station* is on the eastern edge of town. The *General Post Office,* open 9–6:30 weekdays, closed Sunday, is one block east of the bridge, on Wine Street. Shops close at 1 P.M. Wednesdays.

Tralee Co. Kerry (pop. 12,289)

HOTELS: ***Benner's,* Castle Street, 50 rooms, 7 p.b.; ***Mount Brandon,* 164 rooms, 164 p.b.

Waterford Co. Waterford (pop. 31,968)

HOTELS: ***1 Ardree,* Water-town. 100 rooms, 100 p.b. *Bridge*, Bridge Street. 35 rooms, 7 p.b. *Maryland House*, The Mall. 28 rooms, 8 p.b.

GUEST HOUSES: *Mandalay House.* 12 rooms, 5 p.b. *Portree House.* Mary St. 12 rooms.

RESTAURANTS: *Tower Hotel Res-taurant*, The Mall. An up-to-date, swinging eating and drinking place, just behind 11th-century Reginald's Tower. There is an in-expensive grill bar in the *Ardree Hotel.*

USEFUL ADDRESSES: The *Irish Tourist Office* is in Reginald's Tower. The *CIE bus station* is on the Quay, and the *train sta-tion* on the other side of the bridge over the Suir. The *Gen-eral Post Office,* open 9–6:30 Monday-Friday, 9–1 Saturday and closed Sunday, is on the Quay. Shops close at 1 P.M. on Thursdays.

Waterville Co. Kerry (pop. 547)

HOTEL: ***1 Waterville Lake*, 102 rooms, 102 p.b. March 15–Dec. 31. New luxurious resort.

Westport Co. Mayo (pop. 2,882)

HOTEL: ***Jury's Hotel.* 56 rooms, 56 p.b.

RESTAURANT: *Asgard.* Excellent for both seafood and snacks. Smoked salmon and oysters are the specialties.

Wexford Co. Wexford (pop. 11,849)

HOTELS: ***Talbot,* Trinity Street. 116 rooms, 90 p.b. ***1 White's,* North Main Street. 100 rooms, 60 p.b. ***Ferrycarrig Castle,* Ferry-carrig Bridge. 40 rooms, 40 p.b.

GUEST HOUSE: *Whitford House,* New Line Rd. 18 rooms, 4 p.b.

USEFUL ADDRESSES: The *Irish Tourist Office* is on Crescent Quay, the *CIE bus* and *train station* at the north end of town. The *General Post Office* (closed Sundays) is on Anne Street. Shops close at 1 P.M. Thursdays.

NORTHERN IRELAND

Belfast Cos. Antrim and Down (pop. 360,150)

HOTELS: ****1 Conway Hotel*, Dunmurry. 78 rooms, 78 p.b.; ****1 Europa*, Great Victoria Street. 200 rooms, 200 p.b. ****1 Culloden Craigavad*, 33 rooms, 33 p.b. ****1 Russell Court*, Lisburn Rd. 200 rooms, 200 p.b. ***Stormont, 587 Upper Newtownards Rd., 66 rooms, 59 p.b. **Windsor, Knocknagoney Road. 30 rooms, 16 p.b. *Beechlawn, Dunmurry. 13 rooms, 2 p.b.

GUEST HOUSES: *Camera House, 44 Wellington Park. 9 rooms. **Forest Park House*, Upper Dunmurry Lane. 12 rooms. *Botanic Lodge, 87 Botanic Avenue. 11 rooms. *Beechdene*, 11 Botanic Avenue. 5 rooms.

RESTAURANTS: In the top-grade hotels (see above). For good, inexpensive meals in the downtown area: *The Skandia*, 8 Callender St., *The Abercorn*, 7 Castle Lane; *Thompson's*, 47 Arthur Street.

SHOPPING: *Irish linen:* any of several stores on College Street, between Fountain Street and Queen Street. Best buys generally: Anderson & McAuley, Donegall Place, and Robinson & Cleaver, Donegall Square North; The Bank Buildings, Castle Place.

USEFUL ADDRESSES: The *Northern Ireland Tourist Office*, 48 High St., the *main N.I.R./Ulsterbus train and bus station*, Great Victoria Street, two blocks west of City Hall: the *General Post Office*, open 9–4:30 Saturdays, closed Sundays, on Royal Avenue.

Enniskillen Co. Fermanagh

HOTELS: *Killyhevlin, Dublin Road. 25 rooms, 15 p.b.; *Manor House, Killadeas. 15 rooms, 7 p.b.

RESTAURANT: *Melvin House*, 2 Townhall Street.

Londonderry Co. Londonderry (pop. 51,850)

HOTELS: ***Broomhill House Hotel*, Limavady Road. 41 rooms, 15 p.b. *Glen House, Eglinton. 6 rooms, 1 p.b.

GUEST HOUSE: *Clarence House*, 15 Northland Rd. 12 rooms.

RESTAURANTS: *Dolphin*, 41 Strand Road. *Counties Steak House*, 24 Waterloo Place; *The Diamond*, Ferryquay Street.

USEFUL ADDRESSES: *Tourist* information is available at the City Council Offices, Limavady Rd., Mon.-Fri. 9–5. The *Ulsterbus station* is two blocks from the Guildhall on Strand Road, the *N.I.R. train station* across the river via Craigavon bridge. The *General Post Office* is one block from the Guildhall on Customs House Street; it is open Mon.-Fri. 9–5:30, Sat. 9–1, and closed Sundays. Shops close at 1 P.M. on Thursdays.